Spies

Michael Frayn was born in September 1933 in the suburbs of London. As a young boy he displayed a talent for music and poetry and, by the time he was a teenager, he knew that he wanted to be a writer of some sort.

After a brief period in the army during which time he served as a Russian interpreter, Michael attended the University of Cambridge. He graduated in 1957 with a degree in 'moral sciences' and then began his writing career. He worked as a reporter and columnist and presented for the BBC in 1994.

Michael is married to the biographer and critic Clare Tomalin.

SPIES

MICHAEL FRAYN

Winner of the *Whitbread Novel of the Year Award* 2002

Heinemann Educational Publishers
Halley Court, Jordan Hill, Oxford OX2 8EJ
Part of Harcourt Education

Heinemann is the registered trademark of Harcourt Educational Limited

© Michael Frayn

First published in 2002
First published in the New Windmill Series in 2005

2

British Library Cataloguing in Publication Data is available
from the British Library on request.

10-digit ISBN: 0 435120 00 X
13-digit ISBN: 978 0 435120 00 9

Front cover photograph by Michael Frayn
Cover design by Forepoint
Typeset by Tek-Art, Croydon, Surrey

Printed in the UK by Clays Ltd, St Ives plc

1

The third week of June, and there it is again: the same almost embarrassingly familiar breath of sweetness that comes every year about this time. I catch it on the warm evening air as I walk past the well-ordered gardens in my quiet street, and for a moment I'm a child again and everything's before me – all the frightening, half-understood promise of life.

It must come from one of the gardens. Which one? I can never trace it. And what is it? It's not like the heartbreaking, tender sweetness of the lime blossom, for which this city's known, or the serene summer happiness of the honeysuckle. It's something quite harsh and coarse. It reeks. It has a kind of sexual urgency to it. And it unsettles me, as it always does. I feel . . . what? A restlessness. A longing to be over the woods at the end of the street and away, away. And yet at the same time I have a kind of homesickness for where I am. Is that possible? I have a feeling that something, somewhere, has been left unresolved, that some secret thing in the air around me is still waiting to be discovered.

Another hint of it as the summer breeze stirs, and I know that the place I should like to be off to is my childhood. Perhaps the home I'm homesick for is still there, after all. I can't help noticing, as I do every summer in late June, when that sweet reek comes, that there are cheap flights to that far-off nearby land. Twice I pick up the phone to book; twice I put it down again. You can't go back, everyone knows that . . . So I'm never going, then? Is that what I'm deciding? I'm getting old. Who knows, this year may be the last chance I'll get . . .

But what *is* it, that terrible, disturbing presence in the summer air? If only I knew what the magic blossom was called, if only I could see it, perhaps I'd be able to identify the source of its power. I suddenly catch it while I'm walking my daughter and her two small children back to their car after their weekly visit.

I put a hand on her arm. She knows about plants and gardening. 'Can you smell it? There . . . now . . . What is it?'

She sniffs. 'Just the pines,' she says. There are tall pines growing in all the sandy gardens, sheltering the modest houses from the summer sun and making our famously good air fresh and exhilarating. There's nothing clean or resinous, though, about the reek I can detect insinuating itself so slyly. My daughter wrinkles her nose. 'Or do you mean that rather . . . vulgar smell?' she says.

I laugh. She's right. It is a rather vulgar smell.

'Liguster,' she says.

Liguster . . . I'm no wiser. I've heard the word, certainly, but no picture comes to mind, and no explanation of the power it has over me. 'It's a shrub,' says my daughter. 'Quite common. You must have seen it in parks. Very dull looking. It always makes me think of depressing Sunday afternoons in the rain.' Liguster . . . No. And yet, as another wave of that shameless summons drifts over us, everything inside me stirs and shifts.

Liguster . . . And yet it's whispering to me of something secret, of some dark and unsettling thing at the back of my mind, of something I don't quite like to think about . . . I wake up in the night with the word nagging at me. Liguster . . .

Hold on, though. Was my daughter speaking English when she told me that? I get down the dictionary . . . No – she wasn't. And as soon as I see what it is in English I can't help laughing again. Of course! How obvious! I'm laughing this time partly out of embarrassment, because a professional translator shouldn't be caught out by such a simple word – and also because, now I know what it is, it seems such a ridiculously banal and inappropriate cue for such powerful feelings.

Now all kinds of things come back to me. Laughter, for a start. On a summer's day nearly sixty years ago. I've never thought about it before, but now there she is again, my friend Keith's mother, in the long-lost green summer shade, her brown eyes sparkling, laughing at something Keith has written. I see why, of

2

course, now that I know what it was, scenting the air all around us.

Then the laughter's gone. She's sitting in the dust in front of me, weeping, and I don't know what to do or what to say. All around us once again, seeping unnoticed into the deepest recesses of my memory, to stay with me for the rest of my life, is that sweet and luring reek.

Keith's mother. She must be in her nineties now. Or dead. How many of the others are still alive? How many of them remember?

What about Keith himself? Does he ever think about the things that happened that summer? I suppose he may be dead, too.

Perhaps I'm the only one who still remembers. Or half-remembers. Glimpses of different things flash into my mind, in random sequence, and are gone. A shower of sparks . . . A feeling of shame . . . Someone unseen coughing, trying not to be heard . . . A jug covered by a lace weighted with four blue beads . . .

And, yes – those words spoken by my friend Keith that set everything off in the first place. It's often hard to remember the exact words that someone uttered half a century ago, but these are easy, because there were so few of them. Six, to be precise. Spoken quite casually, like the most passing of remarks, as light and insubstantial as soap bubbles. And yet they changed everything.

As words do.

I suddenly have the feeling that I should like to think about all this at some length, now I've started, and to establish some order in it all, some sense of the connections. There were things that no one ever explained. Things that no one even said. There were secrets. I should like to bring them out into the daylight at last. And I sense the presence still, even now that I've located the source of my unrest, of something at the back of it all that remains unresolved.

I tell my children I'm going to London for a few days.

'Do we have a contact for you there?' asks my well-organised daughter-in-law.

'Memory Lane, perhaps,' suggests my son drily. We are evidently all speaking English together. He can sense my restlessness.

'Exactly,' I reply. 'The last house before you go round the bend and it turns into Amnesia Avenue.'

I don't tell them that I'm following the track of a shrub that flowers for a few weeks each summer, and destroys my peace.

I certainly don't tell them the name of the shrub. I scarcely like to name it to myself. It's too ridiculous.

2

Everything is as it was, I discover when I reach my destination, and everything has changed.

Nearly half a century has passed since I last stepped out of a train at this little wooden station, but my feet carry me with a kind of effortless, dreamlike inevitability down the sloping station approach to the quietly busy mid-afternoon main road, left towards the muddled little parade of shops, and left again by the letter box into the long, straight, familiar avenue. The main road's full of fussy new traffic arrangements, the shops have impersonal new commercial names and frontages, and the stringy prunus saplings I remember along the verges of the avenue are now wise and dignified trees. But when I turn the corner once again, off the avenue into the Close . . .

There it is, as it always was. The same old quiet, sweet, dull ordinariness.

I stand on the corner, looking at it, listening to it, breathing it in, not sure whether I'm moved to be here again after all this time, or whether I'm quite indifferent.

I walk slowly up to the little turning circle at the end. The same fourteen houses sit calmly complacent in the warm, dull summer afternoon, exactly as they always did. I walk slowly back to the corner again. It's all still here, exactly as it always was. I don't know why I should find this so surprising. I wasn't expecting anything different. And yet, after fifty years . . .

As the first shock of familiarity subsides, though, I begin to see that everything's not really as it was at all. It's changed completely. The houses have become tidy and tedious, their disparate architectural styles somehow homogenised by new porches and lamps and add-on timbering. I remember each of them as being a world unto itself, as different from all the others as the people who occupied them. Each of them, behind its screen

5

of roses or honeysuckle, of limes or buddleia, was a mystery. Now almost all that luxuriant growth has vanished, and been replaced by hard standing and cars. More cars queue silently along the kerb. The fourteen separate kingdoms have coalesced into a kind of landscaped municipal car park. The mysteries have all been solved. There's a polite, international scent of fast-growing evergreens in the air. But of that wild, indecent smell that lured me here – even on this late June day not a trace remains.

I look up at the sky, the one feature of every landscape and townscape that endures from generation to generation and century to century. Even the sky has changed. Once the war was written across it in a tangled scribble of heroic vapour trails. There were the upraised fingers of the searchlights at night, and the immense coloured palaces of falling flares. Now even the sky has become mild and bland.

I hesitate on the corner again. I'm beginning to feel rather foolish. Have I come all this way just to walk up the road and back, and smell the cypress hedges? I can't think what else to do, though, or what else to feel. I've come to the end of my plans.

And then I become aware of the atmosphere changing around me, as if the past were somehow rematerialising out of the air itself.

It takes me a moment to locate the cause. It's a sound – the sound of an unseen train, muffled and distant at first, then bursting into the clear as it emerges from the cutting through the high ground behind the houses at the top of the Close, just like the train I arrived on twenty minutes earlier. It passes invisibly along the open embankment behind the houses on the left-hand side of the street, then crosses the hollowness of a bridge and slows towards the station beyond.

As this familiar sequence of sounds unrolls, the whole appearance of the Close shifts in front of my eyes. The house on the left-hand corner here, the one I'm standing outside, becomes the Sheldons, the house on the opposite corner the Hardiments. I begin to hear other sounds. The endless clacking of Mr Sheldon's shears unseen behind the high beech hedge, now vanished. The endless scales played by the Hardiments' pale children from gloomy rooms behind the screen of neatly pleached limes (still there). I know, if I turn my head, I shall see further along the street the Geest twins playing some complex skipping game together, their identical pigtails identically bouncing . . . and in the Averys' drive an oily confusion of Charlie and Dave and the constituents of a dismantled three-wheeler . . .

But of course what I'm looking at now is No. 2, next to the Hardiments. Even this appears curiously like all the other houses now, in spite of the fact that it's attached to No. 3 – the only semi-detached pair in the Close. It seems to have acquired a name: Wentworth. It was just a number when I lived in it, and scarcely even a number, since the plate on the gatepost had been creosoted over. There's still something faintly embarrassing about it, though, in spite of its grand new name, and its fresh white render, and the iron control exercised over its front garden by paving stones and impersonal-looking ground cover. Beneath the clean smoothness of the render I can almost see the old cracked and watermarked grey. Through the heavy flags sprout the ghosts of the promiscuous muddle of unidentified shrubs that my father never tended, and the little patch of bald lawn. Our house was made even more shameful by the partner it's yoked to, which was in an even worse state than ours because the Pinchers' garden was a dump for abandoned furniture warped by the rain, and offcuts of lumber and metal that Mr Pincher had stolen from work. Or so everyone in the street believed. Perhaps it was just because of the name, it occurs to me now. In any case the Pinchers were the undesirable elements in the Close – even less desirable than we were, and the terrible connectedness of our houses brought us down with them.

This is what I see as I look at it now. But is that the way that he sees it at his age? I mean the awkward boy who lives in that unkempt house between the Hardiments and the Pinchers – Stephen Wheatley, the one with the stick-out ears and the too-short grey flannel school shirt hanging out of the too-long grey flannel school shorts. I watch him emerge from the warped front door, still cramming food into his mouth from tea. Everything about him is in various shades of grey – even the elastic belt, striped like the hatband of an old-fashioned boater, and fastened with a metal snake curled into the shape of an S. The stripes on the belt are in two shades of grey, because he's entirely monochrome, and he's monochrome because this is how I recognise him now, from the old black-and-white snaps I have at home, that my grandchildren laugh at in disbelief when I tell them it's me. I share their incredulity. I shouldn't have the slightest idea what Stephen Wheatley looks like if it weren't for the snaps, or ever guess that he and I were related if it weren't for the name written on the back.

In the tips of my fingers, though, even now, I can feel the delicious serrated texture of the snake's scaliness.

Stephen Wheatley . . . Or just plain Stephen . . . On his school reports S. J. Wheatley, in the classroom or the playground just plain Wheatley. Strange names. None of them seems quite to fit him as I watch him now. He turns back, before he slams the front door, and shouts some inadequate insult with his mouth full in response to yet another supercilious jibe from his insufferable elder brother. One of his grubby tennis shoes is undone and one of his long grey socks has slipped down his leg into a thick concertina; I can feel in my fingertips, as clearly as the scaliness of the snake, the hopeless bagginess of the failed garter beneath the turned-down top.

Does he know, even at that age, what his standing is in the street? He knows precisely, even if he doesn't know that he knows it. In the very marrow of his bones he understands that there's something not quite right about him and his family, something that doesn't quite fit with the pigtailed Geest girls and the oil-stained Avery boys, and never will.

He doesn't need to open the front gate because it's open already, rotted drunkenly away from the top hinge. I know where he's going. Not across the road to see Norman Stott, who might be all right if it weren't for his little brother Eddie; there's something wrong with Eddie – he keeps hanging around, drooling and grinning and trying to touch you. Not to the Averys or the Geests. Certainly not to see Barbara Berrill, who's as sly and treacherous as most girls are, and who seems even more dislikeable now that his brother Geoff has taken to greasing his hair and hanging around in the twilight smoking cigarettes with her elder sister Deirdre. The Berrill girls' father is away in the army, and everyone says they're running wild.

Stephen's already crossing over the road, as I knew he would, too preoccupied even to turn his head to look for traffic – but then of course in the middle of the war there's no traffic to look for, apart from the occasional bicycle and the slow-plodding horses that draw the floats of the milkman and baker. He's walking slowly, his mouth slightly open, lost in some kind of vague daydream. What do I feel about him as I watch him now? Mostly, I think, an itch to take him by the shoulders and shake him, and tell him to wake up and stop being so . . . so *unsatisfactory*. I'm not the first person, I recall, to have this itch.

I follow him past Trewinnick, the mysterious house where the blackout curtains are always drawn, with a garden decaying behind a cold northern forest of dark firs. Trewinnick isn't shameful, though, like our house and the Pinchers'; its gloomy introversion has a sinister allure. No one knows the name of the people who live here, or even how many of them there are. Their faces are swarthy, their clothes are black. They come and go in the hours of darkness, and keep the blackout drawn in the light.

It's the house next door that he's on his way to; No. 9. Chollerton. The Haywards. He opens the white wicket gate on its well-oiled hinges and closes it carefully behind him. He walks up the neat red brick path that curves through the rose beds, and lifts the wrought iron knocker on the heavy oak front door. Two respectful thumps, not too loud, dampened by the solidity of the oak.

I wait outside the gate and discreetly inspect the house. It's changed less than most of the others. The mellow red brick is still well pointed, the woodwork of the window frames and gables and garage doors as flawlessly white as when Mr Hayward used to paint them himself, in white overalls as clean as the paintwork, whistling, whistling, from morning to night. The red brick path still curves through the rose beds, and the edges of the beds are as geometrically sharp as they used to be. The front door's still unpainted oak, and still pierced by a little diamond-shaped window of spun glass. The name discreetly announced by the weathered copper plate beside the door is still Chollerton. Here at any rate the past has been preserved, in all its perfection.

Stephen waits at the front door. Now, too late, he becomes aware of his appearance. He pulls up the sagging sock, and bends down to tie the untied tennis shoe. But already the door's opening a foot or two, and a boy of Stephen's age stands framed in the darkness of the house beyond. He, too, is wearing a grey flannel shirt and grey flannel shorts. His shirt, though, is not too short, his shorts are not too long. His grey socks are neatly pulled up to half an inch below his knees, and his brown leather sandals are neatly buckled.

He turns his head away. I know what he's doing. He's listening to his mother ask who it is at the door. He's telling her it's Stephen. She's telling him either to ask him in or else to go out and play, but not to hang around on the doorstep, half in and half out.

Keith opens the door completely. Stephen hurriedly scuffs his feet over the metal bars of the shoe scraper, then again over the doormat inside, and the sock with the failed garter slips back down. The door closes behind him.

This is where the story began. At the Haywards. On the day when Keith, my best friend, first pronounced those six simple words that turned our world inside out.

I wonder what it's like inside that front door now. The first thing you saw then, even as the door swung open, was a polished oak hall stand, with clothes brushes, shoe horns and button hooks hanging from it, and a rack for sticks and umbrellas. Then, as you went inside, dark oak panelling, with two matching watercolours of the Trossachs by Alfred Hollings RA, and two china plates covered with blue pagodas and little blue rice-hatted figures crossing little blue footbridges. Between the doors into the living room and the dining room stood a grandmother clock that chimed the quarters, in and out of sequence with the clocks in other rooms, filling the house four times an hour with ethereal, ever-changing music.

And in the middle of it all, my friend Keith. The picture's no longer monochrome, evidently, because now I can see the colours of our belts. Keith's, also fastened with a metal snake curled into the shape of an S, has two yellow bands on the black background, mine two green bands. We're socially colour-coded for ease of reference. Yellow and black are the colours of the right local preparatory school, where all the boys are going to take, and pass, the Common Entrance exam to a public school, and where everyone has his own cricket bat, his own boots and pads, and a special long bag to put them in. Green and black are the colours of the wrong school, where half the boys are gangling oafs like my brother Geoff, who have already taken Common Entrance and failed, and where we play cricket with splintered communal bats – some of us wearing brown gym shoes and our ordinary grey shorts.

I was acutely aware, even then, of my incomprehensible good fortune in being Keith's friend. Now I think about it with adult hindsight it seems more surprising still. Not just his belt but everything about him was yellow and black; everything about me was plainly green and black. He was the officer corps in our two-man army. I was the Other Ranks – and grateful to be so.

We had a great many enterprises and projects in hand, and in all of them he was the leader and I was the led. I see now that he was only the first in a whole series of dominant figures in my life whose disciple I became. His authority was entirely warranted by his intellectual and imaginative superiority. It was Keith, not me, who'd devised the overhead cableway that connected our two houses, along which messages could be catapulted back and forth, like bills and change in the local grocers, and who'd gone on to develop the amazing underground railway, operated by pneumatic pressure, like another cash system we'd seen on expeditions to a nearby department store, through which we could ourselves pass swiftly and effortlessly back and forth, unobserved by the rest of the neighbourhood. Or, at any rate, the cableway and pneumatic tubes along which we and our messages *would* pass, as soon we put the plans into effect.

It was Keith who'd discovered that Trewinnick, the mysterious house next to his with the perpetually drawn blackout, was occupied by the Juice, a sinister organisation apparently behind all kinds of plots and swindles. It was Keith who'd discovered, one Sunday evening on the railway embankment behind the houses, the secret passageway through which the Juice came and went. Or would have discovered in another moment or two, if his father hadn't ordered him to be home in time to pipeclay his cricket boots, ready for school in the morning.

So now Keith and Stephen are standing in the hall, amidst the darkness of the panelling and the gleam of the silver and the delicate chiming of the clocks, deciding what they're going to do this afternoon. Or rather Stephen's waiting for Keith to decide. He may have some chore imposed by his father, which Stephen will be allowed to help with. Maintaining his bicycle, for instance, or sweeping the floor around his father's workbench in the garage. The bicycle in particular requires a great deal of maintenance, because Keith cycles to school each day, and he has a special sports model which has to be kept oiled with special oil, and cleaned with special cleaners until its green frame gleams and its chromium handlebars and rims and three-speed hub glitter in the sun. Cycling's plainly the right way to go to school; the bus which Stephen catches each day at the cracked concrete bus stop on the main road is plainly the wrong way. Green's the right colour for a bicycle, just as it's the wrong one for a belt or a bus.

Or they might be going upstairs to shut themselves away in Keith's playroom. His playroom's as well ordered as the rest of the house. There are no stupid brothers or sisters to take up space and confuse everything, as there are in Stephen's house and all the other houses in the Close where there are children. All Keith's toys are his own, neatly ranged in drawers and cupboards, often in the boxes they came in. There's a deliciously rightful scent of watchmaker's oil from all the solidly engineered clockwork racing cars and speedboats. There are elaborate mechanical constructions, properly assembled from construction sets, with intermeshing cogwheels and ratchets and worm gears, and perfect scale models of Spitfires and Hurricanes properly built from kits, with celluloid canopies, and rectractable undercarriages set in bellies of the most exquisite duck-egg blue. In some of the drawers are battery-powered gadgets – torches that shine in three different colours, and little optical instruments that pass light through lenses and prisms – all of them in actual working condition. There's a shelf of boys' stories in which desert islands are colonised, missions flown in biplanes, and secret passages discovered. There's another shelf of books that tell you how to build a superheterodyne wireless set out of empty cigar boxes, and how to make an egg turn into a silk handkerchief.

If it's fine, and his father hasn't just cut the lawn, they might be going out to play in the garden. They're constructing a railway system which runs from the lowlands of the flower beds behind the garage up into the high mountain passes of the air-raid shelter, where spectacular bridges carry it over breathtaking gorges, then through the dangerous bandit country in the kitchen garden, and on down to the important industrial complex and dock installations behind the cucumber frame. Or will do, as soon as Keith has secured all the necessary way leaves from his father.

They might go out for a walk, up to the golf course, perhaps, where Keith has seen some strange wild animal, a kind of talking monkey, hiding among the gorse bushes, or to the smallholdings in Paradise, where he once saw a crashed German plane with the pilot sitting dead in the cockpit. As they walk they talk about their plans to build a man-carrying glider that can be launched from the roof, or a real car with a real steering wheel. The glider and the car have of course been designed by Keith, but the car's a project in which Stephen's actively involved, because it's to be powered by dozens of old clockwork motors not taken from Keith's inviolable toys but cannibalised from the ample supply of broken ones in Stephen's muddled toy cupboard.

There are a great many projects in hand and a great many mysteries to be investigated. One possibility, though, is too outlandish ever to be mooted – the idea of going to play at Stephen's house. What would be the point? There's no great intercontinental railway being driven through the uninteresting savannahs of *his* back garden, and the idea never crosses Stephen's mind of introducing anyone, least of all Keith, to the room in which he and Geoff not only play but sleep and do their homework. The presence of the two beds is unsuitable enough; Keith's bedroom is quite separate from his playroom. Worse is what's in and on and around the beds – a hopeless tangle of string and plasticine and electric flex and forgotten socks and dust, of old cardboard boxes of mouldering butterflies and broken birds' eggs left over from abandoned projects in the past.

I try to imagine the impossible happening, and Keith asking his mother if he might play at Stephen's house . . . I laugh at the thought. His mother's reclining on the sofa in the sitting room, looking up from her library book. She raises her perfectly plucked eyebrows a quarter of an inch. What is she going to say?

Actually I know precisely what she's going to say: 'I think you'd better ask Daddy about that, darling.'

And what would Daddy say, if Keith somehow found reason and courage enough to persist with this preposterous request? Would he actually turn to look at Stephen for once, in sheer astonishment at the effrontery of the invitation? Of course not. Nor would he reply to the question. He'd simply say something like 'Have you oiled your cricket bat yet, old chap?' And that would be that; they'd go to the kitchen, ask Mrs Elmsley to give them a newspaper to spread over the floor, and they'd oil his cricket bat.

What puzzles me now I look back on it is that Keith's parents had ever allowed their son to build underground tunnels and overhead cable cars to Stephen's house, to go birdsnesting and monkey hunting with him, to invite him to play with his perfectly cared-for toys and help clean his special sports bicycle. It's possible that his father had simply never noticed Stephen's existence, but his mother certainly had. She didn't speak to him personally, but she'd sometimes address him and Keith collectively, as 'you two' or 'chaps'. 'Would you two like a glass of milk?' she might say in the middle of the morning, looking at Keith. Or: 'Come on, chaps. Time to pack up your toys.' Sometimes she'd commission Keith to say something to Stephen individually on her behalf: 'Darling, doesn't Stephen have homework to do . . .? Keith, precious, do you want to invite Stephen to stay to tea?'

She spoke softly and smilingly, with a kind of calm amusement at the world and no excessive movement of her lips. She spent a lot of the day with her feet up on the sofa, or resting in her bedroom, and rested is how she always seemed. She'd appear in the doorway of the playroom, rested, calm, and composed, to announce that she was going down the road to Auntie Dee's, or to the shops. 'You boys will be all right, won't you? You've got things to keep you occupied?' If she wasn't going to the shops or Auntie Dee's she'd be going to the post. She posted letters, it sometimes seemed to Stephen, several times a day.

Keith's father, on the other hand, spent the day working. Not in some unseen office, like Stephen's father and everybody else's father who wasn't away in the Services, but in the garden and the kitchen garden, and around the house, for ever digging and dunging, and trimming and pruning, for ever undercoating and painting, and wiring and rewiring, for ever making perfection yet more perfect. Even the chickens at the bottom of the garden lived irreproachably elegant lives, parading haughtily about a spacious kingdom defined by rectilinear walls of gleaming wire mesh, and retiring to lay clean brown eggs in a hen house where the familiar smells of feed and droppings mingled tastefully with the scent of fresh creosote without and fresh whitewash within.

The headquarters of Keith's father's operations, though, were the garage. The double doors at the front were never opened, but there was a small door in the side, just across the yard from the kitchen, and occasionally, standing behind Keith when he had to go and ask his father for permission to walk on the lawn, or lay out railway track on the paths, Stephen would catch a glimpse of the wonderful private kingdom inside. Keith's father would be intent upon some piece of wood or metal held fast in the great vice on his workbench, dextrously filing or sawing or planing; or sharpening his great range of chisels on a rotary grindstone; or searching in the hundred tidy drawers and pigeonholes above and around the bench for exactly the right grade of glass paper, exactly the right gauge of screw. A characteristic scent hung in the air. What was it? Sawdust, certainly, and machine oil. Swept concrete, perhaps. And car.

The car was another perfection – a small family saloon with constellations of chromium-plated fitments glittering in the darkness of the garage, its bodywork and engine spotlessly maintained in constant readiness for the end of the war, when there would be petrol to run it again. Sometimes the only part of Keith's father to be seen was his legs, projecting from a pool of light underneath the car, as he carried out the full regular schedule of checks and oil changes. All it was missing was its wheels. It stood in perfect immobility on four carefully carpentered wooden chocks, to prevent its being commandeered, as Keith explained, by invading Germans. The wheels themselves were hung neatly on the wall, alongside a picnic hamper, tennis rackets in wooden presses, deflated airbeds and rubber rings – all the apparatus of a forgotten life of leisure which had been suspended, like so many things, for the Duration, that great overarching condition shaping all their lives in so many different ways.

Stephen once plucked up courage to ask Keith privately if the Germans, with the evil ingenuity for which they were notorious, might not take the wheels down from the wall and put them back on the car. Keith explained to him that the wheel nuts which secured them were locked away in a secret drawer by his father's bedside, together with the revolver with which he'd been armed when he was an officer in the Great War, and with which he was going to give any invading Germans this time a nasty surprise.

Keith's father worked and worked – and as he worked he whistled. He whistled as richly and effortlessly as a songbird, an infinitely complex, meandering tune that never reached a resting place any more than his work did. He rarely found a moment to speak. When he did, the words were quick and dry and impatient. 'Door – paint – wet,' he'd inform Keith's mother. If he was in a good mood he'd address Keith as 'old chap'. Sometimes this would become 'old boy', which had imperative overtones: 'Bike away in the shed, old boy.' Occasionally, though, his lips drew back to form what appeared to be a smile, and he'd call Keith 'old bean'. 'If that toy aeroplane of yours touches the greenhouse, old bean,' he'd smile, 'I'll cane you.' Keith evidently believed him. So did Stephen; there was a selection of canes waiting among the sticks and umbrellas on the rack in the hall. Stephen he never addressed at all – never so much as looked at. Even if it was Stephen who was threatening the damage to the greenhouse, it was Keith who was 'old bean' and Keith who'd get caned, because Stephen didn't exist. But then Stephen never spoke to him either, or even looked directly at him, whether he was smiling or not; perhaps because he was too frightened to, or perhaps because if you're non-existent you can't.

There were other reasons why Keith's father inspired respect. He'd won a medal in the Great War, Keith had told Stephen, for killing five Germans. He'd run them through with a bayonet, though exactly how his father had managed to attach a bayonet to the famous revolver Stephen didn't have the courage to ask. There the bayonet still was, though, chillingly bouncing on Keith's father's khaki-trousered buttock every weekend as he marched off in his Home Guard uniform; though it wasn't really the Home Guard that he was going to, as Keith had explained – it was to special undercover work for the Secret Service.

The Haywards were impeccable. And yet they tolerated Stephen! He was very possibly the only person in the Close who ever set foot inside their home, or even in their garden. I try to imagine Norman Stott clumping about Keith's playroom . . . or Barbara Berrill being invited to tea . . . My imagination flounders. I can't make it see even perfectly respectable and self-contained children like the Geest twins, or the pale musicians from No. 1, playing a decorous game of he among the rose beds. I can't picture any of the grown-ups there, for that matter. I stand behind Keith in my mind as he taps at the door of the sitting room . . . 'Come in,' says his mother's voice, scarcely even raised. He opens the door to reveal, politely taking tea with his mother – who? Not Mrs Stott or Mrs Sheldon, obviously. Not my mother (think of *that*, now!). Not Mrs Pincher . . .

No one. Not even Mrs Hardiment or Mrs McAfee.

But then it's impossible to imagine Keith's mother at any of the other houses in the Close.

Except at Auntie Dee's.

Auntie Dee was yet another amazing ornament of the Hayward family.

She lived three doors down, on the same side of the street, almost opposite Stephen's house, behind chocolate-brown half-timbering and flowering almond. My mother and the rest of the street knew her as Mrs Tracey. Keith's mother was tall; Auntie Dee was short. Keith's mother was unhurried and calmly smiling; Auntie Dee was always in a rush, and smiling not calmly at all, but with a reckless display of white teeth and cheerfulness. Keith's mother was back and forth to the shops all the time to get things for Auntie Dee as well as herself, because Auntie Dee was so tied by little Milly and when she wasn't shopping she was in and out of Auntie Dee's looking after Milly while Auntie Dee went.

Sometimes Keith's mother would send Keith down the road in her place, carrying two or three new-laid eggs from that model hen house at the end of the garden, or a newspaper full of freshly cut spring greens, and Stephen would go with him. Auntie Dee's unguarded smile would light up as soon as she opened the door to us, and she'd speak, not just to Keith, but quite directly to both of us, as if I existed just as much as Keith did. 'Hello, Keith! You've had your hair cut! How smart! Hello, Stephen! Your Mummy said you and Geoff had both had terrible snuffles. Are you better now . . .? Oh, I'm so glad! Sit down and play with Milly for a moment while I see if I can find you a slice of cake each.'

And Keith and I would sit awkwardly in the sitting room, amidst the muddle of baby toys on the floor, looking disapprovingly at Milly as she brought us her dolls and picture books, and tried to climb into our laps, as smiling and trustful as her mother. The house was almost as untidy as my own home. The back garden, outside the French windows, was even worse. The grass on the untended lawn was as high as the rusting croquet hoops left over from earlier summers. Keith always had one of his father's disapproving looks on his face while we were in Auntie Dee's house, his eyelids slightly lowered, his lips pursed, as if he were about to start whistling. As I understood it, though, this was no reflection upon his aunt's perfect aunt-likeness. Aunts were supposed to be welcoming, cheerful, and untidy. They were supposed to have little children who smiled at you and tried to climb into your lap. His disapproving look was simply the look that a properly brought-up nephew was supposed to have in an aunt's house. It was further evidence of his family's unshakeable correctness.

In any case, there was a reason for the untidiness. Auntie Dee and even the untidiness itself glowed with a kind of sacred light, like a saint and his attributes in a religious painting, because they reflected the glory of Uncle Peter.

There was a photograph of Uncle Peter in a silver frame on the mantelpiece, smiling the same recklessly open smile as Auntie Dee, his peaked RAF officer's cap set at an angle that echoed the recklessness of the smile. The Berrill girls' father was away in the army somewhere, the McAfees' son was doing his bit in the Far East. But no one had an absent relative who could compare with Uncle Peter. He was a bomber pilot, and he'd flown on special missions over Germany so dangerous and so secret that Keith could only hint at them. Around the photograph were silver cups he'd won at various sports. On the shelves were rows of the adventure stories he'd kept from his boyhood, which Keith was sometimes allowed to borrow. His very absence was a kind of presence. He was manifest in the little silver brooch that Auntie Dee always had pinned to her breast, that showed the three famous initials on a blue enamel background, with the famous wings outspread around them and the famous crown above. You felt his cheerful bravery in Auntie Dee's own brave cheerfulness, his careless disregard for danger in the very untidiness of the house and the neglect of the garden.

It was only Keith's mother who went to Auntie Dee's, never his father. And Auntie Dee never went to Keith's house. The only time I saw Milly's pushchair waiting outside Keith's parents' front door was later – and I knew at once that something was wrong.

Not that there seemed to me anything strange about this lopsided arrangement at the time. The ways of the Haywards were no more open to questioning or comprehension than the domestic arrangements of the Holy Family. Perhaps not even Auntie Dee, in spite of Uncle Peter, was quite up to the standards demanded by God the father.

Only one guest was always welcome at Keith's house: teapot-eared Stephen, with the half-open mouth and the grimy tennis shoes. Didn't Stephen love his own family, then? Didn't he appreciate at the time the qualities that he discovered in them later, and that affected him more and more deeply as he got older?

I don't think he ever thought about whether he loved them or not. They were his family, and that was all there was to it. I suppose he appreciated some of their qualities, because he had some kind of subconscious understanding that his disadvantages in life were a necessary condition of the enthralling difference between Keith's status in the world and his own. How could Stephen have admired Keith's effortless good fortune in being unencumbered with a brother, if he hadn't had to put up with one himself, if he hadn't had to listen to him trying out his new oaths all the time ('God in heaven', 'Jesus wept') and calling everything hell's own boring? Would he have perceived the grace and serenity of Keith's mother quite so clearly if his own hadn't spent most of the day in a faded apron, sighing and anxious, apparently unable to think about anything except Geoff's swearing and Stephen's whereabouts, and the filthy state of their room? Would even Uncle Peter have been quite such a perfect uncle if Stephen himself hadn't had to make do with a handful of obscure aunts in flowered dresses?

Stephen's father and Keith's presented a particularly piquant contrast. The presence of Stephen's father was scarcely noticeable. He was out at an office somewhere all day and often all evening, doing a job, too dull to describe, connected with controls on building materials. Once he'd been away on some business trip in the North for a whole year, and no one had ever talked about it or even noticed particularly. And even when he was at home he didn't whistle that terrifying whistle, he didn't call Stephen 'old bean' and threaten to cane him. He said very little. He often seemed like some mild-natured furry animal. He'd sit for hours at the dining-room table, with papers and files spread out in front of him, and a pair of reading glasses on the end of his nose, or else collapse into one of the scuffed armchairs in the lounge and silently doze through obscure concerts on the wireless that nobody else wanted to hear. He'd loosen his tie, and quantities of disorganised dark hair on his chest would come sprouting out of the open neck of his shirt. Then his head would sink and present the world with yet more disorganised hair, dotted in irregular tufts about the infertile landscape of his scalp. Even the backs of his hands had coarse dark hair on them – even the gaps between his turn-ups and his crumpled socks. His appearance was as unsatisfactory as Stephen's.

Sometimes, when he was awake, he'd ask Stephen and Geoff politely what they'd been doing with themselves. He spoke slowly and carefully, as if he thought they might not understand him. And when he did finally become exasperated with them, the worst punishment he could contrive was a generalised swipe at their heads, which they effortlessly ducked. The cause of the exasperation was usually their room, and the muddle it was in, which he sometimes referred to as *coodle-moodle*. There was something embarrassingly private about this; no one else in the Close had ever uttered such a word. If Stephen argued back, and tried to insist that not clearing up the room saved time for more important matters such as homework, his father would occasionally produce an even more eccentric word: '*shnick-shnack*'. Stephen once repeated this to Keith, on perhaps the only occasion that he didn't entirely believe something Keith had told him. 'You know Auntie Dee's baby?' said Keith. 'She was grown from a seed.' 'Shnick-shnack,' said Stephen uncertainly, and he knew from the look on Keith's face that he'd said the wrong thing once again.

I also remember the time Stephen told his father about the Juice moving into Trewinnick. His father gave him one of his long, thoughtful looks.

'It's true,' said Stephen. 'Keith said.'

His father laughed. 'Oh, Keith said. In that case we need inquire no further. Shnick-shnack.'

No, Stephen must have loved his family, because loving your family was the ordinary arrangement in life, and everything in Stephen's family, or so it seemed to him, even the coodle-moodle, was quite extraordinarily ordinary. But where he longed to be was at Keith's house. And what he loved most at Keith's house was being invited to tea.

Those teas! At once I taste the chocolate spread on the thick plank of bread. I feel in my fingertips the diamond pattern incised in the tumblers of lemon barley. I see the shining dark table in the dining room, where Keith and I are allowed to sit on our own, unfolding napkins from the bone napkin rings, helping ourselves from the tall jug of lemon barley covered by a lace weighted with four blue beads.

Between the silver candlesticks on the mantelpiece is a silver ashtray propped upright and inscribed 'WWLTC. Senior Mixed Doubles. Runners-up – W. P. Hayward and R. J. Whitman, 27 July 1929.' W. P. Hayward and R. J. Whitman, as Keith long ago explained, were his parents before they were married, and the WWLTC was the Wimbledon World Lawn Tennis Club. They would have been world champions if they hadn't been somehow cheated out of it by another couple who were members of the same sinister organisation now entrenched in Trewinnick. On the sideboard, between two cut-glass decanters, is Uncle Peter, in another silver frame. His smile's more restrained here in Keith's parents' house, and his officer's cap is straight. Every detail is sharp on the eagle, crown, and thickly embroidered laurel leaves above the peak, and on the pilot's wings above his left breast pocket.

At the end of an afternoon when Stephen has stayed to tea, Keith taps on the sitting-room door, and ushers him into his mother's presence to make his farewell speech. Balanced on an occasional table by the sofa is a tea tray of her own, with a silver teapot, a silver milk jug, and a little silver box containing tiny pills of saccharine. She's on the sofa, with her feet tucked up beneath her, reading her library book. Or she's sitting at a desk in the far corner, writing the letters she posts so copiously, watched by another dozen or so silver-framed family photographs ranged over the desk in front of her. Stephen doesn't dare look directly at anything in this holy place. Keith's mother glances up and smiles. 'Oh, is Stephen going home?' she asks Keith. 'You must invite him again another time.'

Stephen steps forward and delivers his speech. 'Thank you for having me,' he mumbles.

'As long as you both had fun together,' she says.

I don't suppose Stephen's words meant very much to him at the time, so let me say them again now, on his behalf, before everything that was going to happen happened. With sincere gratitude, and a sense of wonder at my good fortune that has grown only stronger over the years. Gratitude not only to Keith's mother, but to Keith himself, to all the others after him whose adjutant and audience I was, and to everyone else who wrote and performed the drama of life in which I had a small, often frightening, but always absorbing part:

Thank you for having me. Thank you, thank you.

So what was the source of that disconcerting perfume?

It wasn't the neat standard roses in the Haywards' front garden, nor the muddle of heaven knows what in ours. It wasn't the limes in front of the Hardiments, or the buddleia at the Stotts and the McAfees, or the honeysuckle at Mr Gort's and the Geests.

I walk slowly back down the street, looking at the houses opposite the Haywards, trying to be sure. It didn't come from No. 6 – that was the Berrills, and a barbed-wire entanglement of overgrown wild roses . . . No. 5 was the Geests . . . At No. 3 we're back to the Pinchers. So it can only have been this one, in between the Geests and the Pinchers, No. 4.

I stop and examine it carefully. The rustic sign on the wrought-iron gate says Meadowhurst, and there's not much garden visible apart from four neat tubs of geraniums and three cars parked on the flagged hard standing. The house itself looks unfamiliar to me. Its whole style is subtly different from all the other houses in the street – it was plainly built much later. Yes, this was the place – our Arcadia, our Atlantis, our Garden of

Eden, the unclaimed territory left after Miss Durrant's house was gutted by a stray German incendiary bomb.

It was called Braemar in those days. Already, when Stephen and all the other children in the Close played there, the brambles and fireweed and dog-roses had begun to conceal the melancholy little landscape of uncleared rubble covering the foundations of the house in which Miss Durrant had lived and died. The whole garden was running wild, like the Berrill girls, and the tall green hedge at the front, which Miss Durrant had kept so rectilinear, and behind which she had maintained her privacy so carefully, had lost its shape and grown into a straggling underwood that closed the entrance to this secret kingdom completely and lost it to the world.

Stephen spent a lot of time concealed in the midst of those unremarkable dull-green bushes that had once been a hedge. He scarcely noticed them, though. Not, at any rate, until some time towards the end of that June, when they came into blossom around him, and half-suffocated him with the coarse sweetness that would pursue him down the years.

I gaze at the four tubs of geraniums and the three cars. Of the bushes now there's no longer a trace. I can't help laughing at myself when I remember what they were, because the species is so commonplace, so despised and ridiculed, so associated with the repression and concealment of all the wild feelings it seems to have released in me. Let me say the name and get it out into the open, once and for all.

The source of all my great unrest is this: plain ordinary privet.

Where the story began, though, was where most of our projects and adventures began – at Keith's house. At the tea table, in fact – I can hear the soft clinking made by the four blue beads that weighted the lace cloth covering the tall jug of lemon barley . . .

No, wait. I've got that wrong. The glass beads are clinking against the glass of the jug because the cover's stirring in the breeze. We're outside, in the middle of the morning, near the chicken run at the bottom of the garden, building the transcontinental railway.

Yes, because I can hear something else, as well – the trains on the real railway, as they emerge from the cutting on to the embankment above our heads just beyond the wire fence. I can see the showers of sparks they throw up from the live rail. The jug of lemon barley isn't our tea – it's our elevenses, waiting with two biscuits each on a tray his mother has brought us out from the house, and set down on the red brick path beside us. It's as she walks away, up the red brick path, that Keith so calmly and quietly drops his bombshell.

When is this? The sun's shining as the beads clink against the jug, but I have a feeling that there's still a trace of fallen apple blossom on the earthworks for the transcontinental railway, and that his mother's worried about whether we're warm enough out there. 'You'll come inside, chaps, won't you, if you get chilly?' May still, perhaps. Why aren't we at school? Perhaps it's a Saturday or a Sunday. No, there's the feel of a weekday morning in the air; it's unmistakable, even if the season isn't. Something that doesn't quite fit here, as so often when one tries to assemble different bits to make a whole.

Or have I got everything back to front? Had the policeman already happened before this?

It's so difficult to remember what order things occurred in – but if you can't remember *that*, then it's impossible to work out which led to which, and what the connection was. What I remember, when I examine my memory carefully, isn't a narrative at all. It's a collection of vivid particulars. Certain words spoken, certain objects glimpsed. Certain gestures and expressions. Certain moods, certain weathers, certain times of day and states of light. Certain individual moments, which seem to mean so much, but which mean in fact so little until the hidden links between them have been found.

Where did the policeman come in the story? We watch him as he pedals slowly up the Close. His appearance has simultaneously justified all our suspicions and overtaken all our efforts, because he's coming to arrest Keith's mother . . . No, no – that was earlier. We're running happily and innocently up the street beside him, and he represents nothing but the hope of a little excitement out of nowhere. He cycles right past all the houses, looking at each of them in turn, goes round the turning circle at the end, cycles back down the street . . . and dismounts in front of No. 12. What I remember for sure is the look on Keith's mother's face, as we run in to tell her that there's a policeman going to Auntie Dee's. For a moment all her composure's gone. She looks ill and frightened. She's throwing the front door open and not walking but running down the street . . .

I understand now, of course, that she and Auntie Dee and Mrs Berrill and the McAfees all lived in dread of policemen and telegraph boys, as everyone did then who had someone in the family away fighting. I've forgotten now what it had turned out to be – nothing to do with Uncle Peter, anyway. A complaint about Auntie Dee's blackout, I think. She was always rather slapdash about it.

Once again I see that look cross Keith's mother's face, and this time I think I see something else beside the fear. Something that reminds me of the look on Keith's face, when his father's discovered some dereliction in his duties towards his bicycle or his cricket gear; a suggestion of guilt. Or is memory being overwritten by hindsight once more?

If the policeman and the look *had* already happened, could they by any chance have planted the first seed of an idea in Keith's mind?

I think now that most probably Keith's words came out of nowhere, that they were spontaneously created in the moment they were uttered. That they were a blind leap of pure fantasy. Or of pure intuition. Or, like so many things, of both.

From those six random words, anyway, came everything that followed, brought forth simply by Keith's uttering them and by my hearing them. The rest of our lives was determined in that one brief moment as the beads clinked against the jug and Keith's mother walked away from us, through the brightness of the morning, over the last of the fallen white blossom on the red brick path, erect, composed, and invulnerable, and Keith watched her go, with the dreamy look in his eye that I remembered from the start of so many of our projects.

'My mother,' he said reflectively, almost regretfully, 'is a German spy.'

3

So, she's a German spy.

How do I react to the news? Do I offer any comment?

I don't think I say anything at all. I think I just look at Keith with my mouth slightly open, as I've done so many times before, waiting to find out what comes next. Am I surprised? Of course I'm surprised – but then I'm often surprised by Keith's announcements. I was surprised when he first told me that Mr Gort, who lives alone at No. 11, was a murderer. But then, when we investigated, we found some of the bones of his victims in the waste ground just beyond the top of his garden.

So I'm surprised, certainly, but not as surprised as I should be now. And of course I'm immediately excited, because I can see all kinds of interesting new possibilities opening up, for hiding and watching in the gloaming, for sending and receiving messages in invisible ink, for wearing the moustaches and beards in Keith's disguises kit, for examining things through Keith's microscope.

I think I feel a brief pang of admiring jealousy for yet another demonstration of his unending good fortune. A father in the Secret Service *and* a mother who's a German spy – when the rest of us can't muster even one parent of any interest!

Does it occur to me to wonder whether his father knows about his mother's activities – or his mother about his father's? Or to reflect on the delicate situation that this clash of loyalties must create in the household? I don't think it does. They're plainly both skilled at concealing their real selves from the world, and they've presumably managed to keep their respective secrets from each other. In any case, how adults behave among themselves is a mystery about which I haven't yet learnt to have any curiosity.

I'm slightly regretful, though. I think of all the lemon barley and chocolate spread I've had from her, all the tolerance, all the intimations of grace and composure. Pleased as I am to have a

German spy to investigate, I should much rather it had turned out to be Mrs Sheldon or Mrs Stott. Or even Keith's father. I could easily believe that Keith's father is a German. Or could have, if I hadn't known about his Secret Service work and his notable attempts to reduce the German population during the Great War.

No, on second thoughts I'm relieved that it's not Keith's father. The idea of keeping watch on *him* is too frightening to contemplate. I see his lips drawn back in the little smile: 'Anyone give you permission to interfere with my secret transmitter, old bean . . .'

Do I ask Keith the first and most obvious question – *how* he knows that she's a spy? Of course not, any more than I've ever asked him how he knows that she's his mother, or that his father's his father. She just is his mother, in the same way that Mrs Sheldon's Mrs Sheldon, and Barbara Berrill's beneath our notice, and my family's slightly disgraceful. Everyone knows that these things are so. They don't have to be explained or justified.

In fact, as I get used to the idea in the days that follow, it begins to make sense of a lot of things. All those letters that his mother writes, for instance. Who are they to? The only human beings the Haywards know, apart from me, are Auntie Dee and Uncle Peter. I suppose they must have other aunts and uncles somewhere – everyone has aunts and uncles somewhere. But mothers write to aunts and uncles a couple of times a year, not every day! You don't need to go out to catch the post twice in one afternoon! If she were sending off reports to the Germans, though . . . Reports on what? Whatever she goes to spy on when she makes all those trips to the shops. The local anti-aircraft defences, probably – the air-raid wardens' post on the corner of the lane to Paradise and the static water tank behind the library. The secret munitions factory on the main road where Mr Pincher pinches his aluminium trims and sheets of plywood.

Mr Pincher himself, for that matter, and all the assistance his activities are giving to the enemy. The strange goings-on at Trewinnick. Careless talk about the whereabouts of Mr Berrill and the McAfees' son. The general state of civilian morale in the Close, as revealed in Mrs Sheldon's complaints about the quality of the meat at Hucknalls and Auntie Dee's carelessness with her blackout. She has her eye on all of us.

It even begins to make sense of a number of things (and this is surely the real test of a new insight) that I hadn't realised didn't make sense before. Why did the Germans drop an incendiary bomb on the Close, out of all the streets around? And why on Miss Durrant's house, out of all the houses in the Close? But if Miss Durrant had found out the truth about Keith's mother, and was about to unmask her . . . And if Keith's mother had realised, and had gone out in the blackout and signalled to them with a torch, to guide them to the target . . .

There's a torch on the table in the Haywards' hall.

I believe another uneasy thought occurs to me, too: that it might help to explain all her incomprehensible niceness to me, all that lemon barley and chocolate spread. It's simply part of her false identity, to conceal her true nature.

Already, within moments of Keith's announcement, while I'm still gaping and long before I've begun to take in the consequences, we've abandoned the transcontinental railway and begun to shadow her. We watch over the banisters as she goes between sitting room and kitchen, talking to Mrs Elmsley about the polishing of the silver and the ailments of Mrs Elmsley's mother. In the stationery cupboard in the playroom we find the exercise book we were going to use to record our observations of birds, until we gave up observing birds for tracking down the ape-like creature on the gold course. Keith crosses out BIRDS and writes LOGBOOK – SECRIT. I have private reservations about the spelling, but keep them to myself, as I do all the other small occasional reservations I have about his authority.

He begins to make a record of our observations. '1053 hrs,' he writes, as we crouch at the top of the stairs, listening to his mother in the hall below. 'Phones. Asks for 8087. Mr Hucknall. 3 muten chops. Not to much fat. By noon.' We flee into the playroom as she comes upstairs . . . halt our investigations and think about something else while she's in the lavatory . . . emerge and follow her downstairs to the kitchen . . . out into the garden to watch her from behind the shed as she takes the familiar steaming, sour-smelling enamel bowl into the chicken run . . . She does far more different things in the course of the morning, now we're taking note of them, than I'd ever realised, with not a single pause to rest or write letters. It's easy to miss how active she is because she does it all in such a smooth, unhurried way – because she does it all so . . . *inconspicuously.*

Yes, there's a sinister unnoticeability about the whole performance, now that we know the truth behind it. There's something clearly *wrong* about her, if you really look at her and listen to her as we now are. You can hear a false note in the specially graceful, specially impersonal way she talks to Mrs Elmsley, to Keith's father, even to the chickens. 'You did remember to dust behind the dining-room clock this time, didn't you, Mrs Elmsley . . .? Ted, darling, do you want anything from the shops? I've got to get a few things for Dee. Awfully good job you're doing with those lettuce seedlings, by the way . . . Now, come on, ladies. No pushing and shoving. A nice orderly queue, please. Ration books ready . . .'

I detect the same falsity in the specially amused tone she uses to Keith and me, when she turns round, on her way back to the house with the empty bowl, and sees us running from cover to cover, from behind the garden shed to behind the pergola, to keep up with her. 'Bang bang!' she says humorously, pointing an imaginary gun at us, as if we were children. 'Got you, the pair of you!' She's pretending to be part of some innocent children's game. And all the time she's a stranger in our midst, watching us with alien eyes.

For the first time I take a good look at Mrs Elmsley. It had never occurred to me before to wonder why she has a moustache and a wart in the middle of her forehead, or why she speaks so softly . . .

Then again, is the 'Mr Hucknall' Keith's mother spoke to on the phone really Mr Hucknall, the familiar bloodstained comedian of the butcher's shop? And even if he is, his connection with a known spy now makes us begin to wonder about *him*. I think of the humorously loud way he sings as he hurls the cuts of meat on to the scale when he's still several feet away from it. 'If you were the only girl in the world . . .' Then tosses the shining brass weights from hand to hand as if they were juggler's clubs. 'And I was the only boy . . .' Then shouts to the cash desk: 'Take two and fourpence off this good lady, Mrs Hucknall. *And* the next, please . . .' Like Keith's mother he's putting on a performance; he's trying to conceal his true nature. Are 'mutton chops' really mutton chops, for that matter? In any case, when the boys arrives on his heavy delivery bicycle just before noon, with the plate saying 'F. Hucknall, Family Butcher' under the crossbar, how do we know that the little white parcel that he takes out of the great basket over the tiny front wheel really contains mutton chops?

Everything that we'd once taken for granted now seems open to question. Even what appears to be happening directly in front of your eyes, you realise when you think about it, turns out to be something you can't actually quite see after all, to involve all kinds of assumptions and interpretations.

By the time Keith's mother tells him to wash his hands for lunch, and I run home for mine, we've assembled a considerable body of evidence in the logbook. As I gulp down my corned beef and boiled potatoes, and tip my swedes into the pig-food bowl, I can't think of anything except the next and more alarming stage of our investigation, planned for this afternoon. While Keith's mother is having her rest upstairs we're going to creep into the sitting room. We're going to take the looking glass that hangs with the clothes brushes and shoehorns in the hall, and we're going to examine the blotter on her desk, because she'll have blotted the letters she writes and left clearly legible traces in mirror writing. If by any chance that doesn't work, we're also going to take the torch from the hall table, to show up the impressions the pen will have left in the surface of the blotting paper.

I'm dimly aware that my mother is fussing away on some familiar theme. I think it's her usual: 'You're not making a nuisance of yourself going over to Keith's house all the time, are you?'

'No,' I mumble, with my mouth full of semolina pudding; not something that Keith would ever do – or me either, if I were at his house.

'You're not going back there this afternoon?'

I don't think I reply to this. I don't think I even look at her. There's something so hopelessly ordinary about her that it's difficult to take account of her existence.

'I should think his mother might like a bit of peace occasionally. She doesn't want you boys round her feet all the time.'

I smile a secret smile to myself. If only she knew!

'Why don't you ask Keith to come and play here for once?'

She doesn't understand anything, and I couldn't begin to explain. I finish my semolina and get down from the table, still swallowing.

'Where are you off to?'

'Nowhere.'

'Not to Keith's house?'

'No.'

Actually I'm not – not yet, because I'm not allowed to arrive there until I'm sure his father has finished lunch. I go out into the street to see if I can find anyone else to play with to pass the time. Norman Stott might be hanging around, hoping I'll also be at a loose end. Or the Geest twins might be out in their front garden, playing one of their endless skipping games. I'm longing to tell someone about the amazing discovery we've made, and the important work we're engaged upon. Or rather, not actually to tell them, but to drop a few oblique and tantalising hints. No, not even to drop hints, but to say nothing about it, and simply know what they don't. I imagine catching one of Wanda and Wendy's fleeting, private, superior smiles to each other, and all the time having a secret of my own, vastly superior to any that they could possibly share. I think of scuffling drearily with Norman, and doing it merely to conceal from him that I've really left such childish time-wasting far behind me.

But everyone's still indoors having lunch. I walk all the way round the empty Close. Even the Avery boys' three-wheeler is sitting abandoned in its oil stains – easy prey, with all three wheels still attached, for any passing German troops. In the absence of anyone else I should for once be prepared to exchange a few words with Barbara Berrill. She's always hanging around when you don't want her, pulling affected girlish faces and making affected girlish gestures. Today I could feel even more agreeably scornful of her than ever – and of course she's nowhere to be seen.

I keep a discreet watch on Keith's house, waiting for his father's whistling, or some other evidence that life has resumed after lunch. Nothing. Silence. Just the self-contained perfection of the house itself, the effortless superiority which the other houses in the Close can only recognise and defer to. And now, unknown to anyone except Keith and myself, it has another advantage over them, a secret importance locked away inside its heart that no one would ever guess at.

What a surprise all the ordinary dull citizens of the Close – my mother, the Berrills, the Geests, the McAfees – are going to be getting very shortly!

It will be an even bigger surprise for Auntie Dee, of course, when she sees the policeman on his bicycle stop at Keith's mother's house, because now there will be no one to look after Milly or do the shopping for her. It's going to be very sad for Keith, too, it occurs to me, after they've taken his mother away, and he and his father are left alone to get on with their lives together. Mrs Elmsley will make his lunch, if she hasn't been arrested herself. But I somehow don't see Mrs Elmsley, with her wart and her moustache, setting out chocolate spread for tea. Will she allow me stay for tea at all?

The consequences of this investigation, I'm beginning to see, are going to be rather sad for all of us. It's not as simple as I'd originally thought.

But then what can we do, if she's a German spy? We have to make sacrifices for the War Effort. We have to endure hardships for the sake of the Duration.

I hear whistling. Round the side of Keith's house I catch a glimpse of his father, heading in the direction of the kitchen garden. I put all feelings of pity behind me, and open their garden gate.

'You chaps have got things to keep you occupied, have you?' says Keith's mother, putting her head round the playroom door on her way to retire for her rest. We nod mutely. 'Just try not to make too much noise, then.'

We never make too much noise. But now we make no noise at all. We sit on the floor in absolute silence, not looking at each other, straining our ears until we hear the soft, well-oiled click of her bedroom door closing. Then we creep downstairs, freezing at every creak of a board or squeak of fingers on banister. Very softly Keith takes down the looking glass from its hook, and picks up the torch from the hall table. Very slowly he turns the handle of the sitting-room door, then pauses again, looking back at the stairs.

The grandmother clock ticks. There's no other sound. I wish I were back at home.

He eases the door open. Inside the room the silence is more absolute still. Every suggestion of sound is absorbed by the thicknesses of the pale green carpet, of the dark green velvet curtains and the matching upholstery. We glide across to the desk as silently as Sioux. The darkness of its polished surface is lit by the gleam of silver and its reflections: a paper knife, a table lighter, a pair of candle snuffers, and the various silver-framed photographs reclining at dignified angles on unseen elbows. Keith opens the two leather-bound wings of the blotter.

A virgin snowfield confronts us, with no trace of blotted mirror writing. He puts the looking glass aside and switches on the torch. He lays it down at the edge of the blotter, in the way that we've read about in various books, so that it casts long shadows like the setting sun, then bends down and peers through the magnifying glass from his stamp-collecting kit. Slowly, systematically, he inches his way from the centre outwards.

I look at the photographs in the silver frames while I wait. From one of them a girl of about the same age as Keith and myself gazes solemnly back at me, slightly out of focus. She's standing in a garden dappled with sunshine, wearing long white gloves that cover her bare arms up to her elbows and a wide-brimmed summer hat several sizes too big for her. It's Keith's mother, I realise uneasily, and she's playing at being the grown-up she has since become. She has a protective arm around another little girl, several years younger, who's holding a doll and looking up at her, trusting but very slightly apprehensive. It's Auntie Dee, playing at being her elder's sister's little girl. There's something almost improper about the sight of them like this, stripped of their protective adulthood, caught out in a childish pretence, and something quite upsetting about Auntie Dee's innocent ignorance of what her older sister will one day become.

Keith straightens up and silently hands me the magnifying glass. I bend over and imitate his methodical slowness. There *are* impressions in the blotting paper, but they're very faint and confused. Some of them might be the shapes of overlaid words. I think I can make out a few odd letters, and perhaps even one or two syllables: 'Thus', possibly, and 'if you'.

Keith whispers in my ear: 'Do you see it?' He points. I peer at the area around his enormous fingernail. I think I can distinguish a figure 8 and a figure 2. Or else a figure 3 and a question mark.

'Code,' whispers Keith.

He makes a note of various letters and digits in the logbook, then closes up the blotter. I feel nothing but relief that the operation's over and that we can get out of the room before his mother wakes up or his father comes back to the house. But Keith puts a restraining hand on my arm; he hasn't finished yet. He softly slides open the long drawer beneath the desktop. His mother goes on gazing at us out of her silver frame as we bend down again to examine its contents.

Headed writing paper . . . envelopes . . . books of tuppenny-halfpenny stamps . . . Everything neatly ordered, with plenty of space . . . An address book . . .

Keith takes out the address book and turns over the pages. The entries are written in a neat, clear hand. Ashtons (cleaners), ABC Stationers . . . Mr and Mrs James Butterworth, Marjorie Beer, Bishop (window cleaner) . . . Who are Mr and Mrs Butterworth and Marjorie Beer? They may be code names, of course . . . Doctor, Dentist . . . There are no more than a handful of names under each letter, and a lot of them seem to be tradesmen. I notice 'Hucknall (Butcher) . . .' No one in the Close as far as I can see, except Mr and Mrs Peter Tracey . . . Keith examines each of the entries through the magnifying glass, and transcribes a few of them into the logbook.

Meanwhile I look at the photographs again. Three laughing figures in tennis whites: Keith's mother and Auntie Dee, with Uncle Peter lounging boyishly between them, and beside them a fourth figure whose lifeless clipped grey hair and grimly ironic smile have already taken on the character I find so alarming. The same four on a beach, with Uncle Peter standing on his head, and Keith's mother and Auntie Dee holding him by his ankles. Then a serious young bride standing in front of a church door, shyly holding her veil back from her face, the long white train of her dress tumbled elaborately down the steps in front of her: Keith's mother, her arm tucked demurely through the arm of a grey tailcoat with an ironic smile above it.

Next to this last one, arranged beside it so as to make a pair, another bride, almost identical with the first, in front of what appears to be the same church door, with the same train tumbled down the same steps. This bride's a little shorter, though, a little bolder looking, a little more up to date in some indefinable way, and the arm she's holding is encased in a shade of grey that I know represents not grey at all but air-force blue, and that belongs to a bridegroom whose hair and smile are both still boyish.

Mother and father, aunt and uncle – all four of them watch us out of the past as we work to penetrate the secrets of the present and dismantle their future.

At the back of the drawer Keith has found a little pocket diary. I feel a fresh wave of alarm. We're not going to look in her *diary*, are we? Diaries are private . . . But already he's opened it, and already I'm looking over his shoulder as he turns the pages.

Again the entries are sparse: 'Doctor . . . Milly's b'day . . . curtains cleaned . . . wedding anniv . . ?' A few seem to be social occasions: 'Bridge Curwens . . . Ted's parents . . . Ted to OH dinner . . ?' A lot of them relate to K. 'K's term starts (blazer cleaned, cricket shirts) . . . K's sports day . . . K to dentist . . ?'

I don't know how Keith notices the first of the secret signs. I realise that he's stopped turning the pages, and brought the diary very close to his eyes, the magnifying glass forgotten. He looks at me. He's wearing the special expression he has when something really important occurs. It's the way he looked at me as the first of the vertebrae emerged from the earth at the end of Mr Gort's garden.

'What?' I whisper. He hands the diary to me, and points to the space for a Friday in January.

It seems at first to be empty. Then I see that there's some kind of handwritten mark, even smaller than the other entries, nestling inconspicuously in the little gap between the date itself and the current phase of the moon: a tiny x.

A strange tingling feeling goes through me. This is something quite different from what we've been recording up to now. Whatever this inconspicuous symbol means, it's plainly something that's not meant to be read or understood by anyone else. We've stumbled across something that's actually secret.

Keith's still looking at me with his special expression, waiting to see how I respond. There's a certain light in his eyes that I don't like. He can see that my courage is beginning to falter again, as it did when he held up the first of the buried vertebrae, and I didn't want to go on digging. His expectations are fulfilled: my interest in continuing with the current investigation, I discover, has suddenly evaporated.

I put the diary back in the drawer.

'We'd better just leave it,' I whisper.

The corner of Keith's mouth registers an almost imperceptible moment of superiority. I remember how often I've been humiliated by him like this in the past. Things start as a game, and then they turn into a test, which I fail.

He takes the diary out of the drawer again, and slowly turns the pages over.

'But if it's something private . . .' I plead.

'Put it in the logbook,' he orders.

He watches as I reluctantly scribble the date, and mark an x against it. I'm halfway to the door before I realise that he's still by the desk, turning over more pages of the diary.

'Something else,' he says. 'A different thing.'

I hesitate. But in the end, of course, I have to go back and look over his shoulder. He points to a Saturday in February. There's a tiny exclamation mark next to the date.

'Make a note of it,' he says.

He turns the pages again. More x's. More exclamation marks. As I record them, a pattern begins to emerge. The x, whatever it is, happens once a month. Sometimes it's crossed out and entered a day or two earlier or later. The exclamation mark, however, has happened only three times so far this year, and at irregular intervals – on a Saturday in January, on another Saturday in March, and on a Tuesday in April. This last date, I'm somehow disturbed to see, is also marked 'wedding anniv.'

A gathering sense of mystery begins to overwhelm my uneasiness. I look at Keith's mother smiling shyly out at us from behind her veil. I can't take it in. She actually *is* a German spy. And not in the way that Mr Gort is a murderer, or that the people who come and go at Trewinnick are members of some sinister organisation. Not in the way that anyone in the street might be a murderer or a German spy. She is quite literally . . . *a German spy*.

We go once again through the list I've written in the logbook. There's something she does once a month. Something she has to keep track of. Some secret thing. What is it?

'She has meetings with someone,' I suggest. 'Secret meetings. They're all planned in advance – only then sometimes the person can't come, so they have to change the date . . .'

Keith watches me, saying nothing. Now I've got my brain started, it's racing faster than his for once.

'Then every now and then something else happens,' I go on slowly. 'Something surprising, something that wasn't planned . . .'

Keith's smiling his little smile, I realise. He's not behind me at all – he's somehow ahead of me again, and simply biding his time to tantalise me.

'The meetings with x,' he whispers finally. 'When are they supposed to happen?'

I feel the skin prickle on the back of my neck. From the sound of his voice there's something eerie coming, but I can't guess what it's going to be. 'Once a month,' I whisper helplessly.

He slowly shakes his head.

'Yes – look. January, February . . .'

He shakes his head again. 'Once every four weeks,' he says.

I'm lost. 'What's the difference?'

He waits, smiling his little smile, while I go through the diary again. I suppose it's true. Each month the date seems to be a little earlier. 'So?'

'Look at the moon,' he whispers.

I go back to the beginning, looking at the phases of the moon next to each of the little x's. Yes, the x's are approximately keeping step with the lunar calendar. Each month the x is close to the same sign, the full black circle. I look up at Keith.

'The night of no moon,' he whispers.

The hairs rise on my neck again. I can see the possibilities now as clearly as he can – the unlit plane landing on the fairway of the golf course, the parachutist falling softly through the perfect darkness . . .

I turn over the pages of the diary. The last x was two nights ago. The next is in twenty-six days' time. After that – nothing. No x's, no exclamation marks.

One last meeting, then, in the dark of the moon . . .

And suddenly the whole house is full of cascading, tangled fairy music. All three clocks are chiming simultaneously.

At the first shimmering tintinnabulations we've already jumped out of our skins, thrown the diary back into the drawer, slammed the drawer shut, and got halfway to the door.

And there's Keith's mother, standing on the threshold, as shocked to find herself face to face with us as we are to find ourselves face to face with her.

'What are you doing in here?' she demands.

'Nothing,' says Keith.

'Nothing,' I confirm.

'Not taking something out of my desk?'

'No.'

'No.'

Did she see us? Does she realise? How long has she been watching us? All three of us stand our ground, not knowing quite how to resolve the situation.

'Why have you got such funny looks on your faces?'

Keith and I glance at each other. It's true – we do have funny looks on our faces. But it's difficult to know what sort of look would be appropriate for talking to someone who we know has just had a secret rendezvous with a German courier. And when we mustn't let her know that we know.

She puts the library book she's holding down on the desk, picks up another, then hesitates, frowning. 'Isn't that your magnifying glass?' she demands. 'And what's the torch doing in here? And the looking glass?'

'We were just playing,' says Keith.

'Well, you know you shouldn't be doing it in here,' she says. 'Why don't you go outside and play?'

Silently Keith puts the magnifying glass in his pocket. Silently we replace the torch and the looking glass. I look back as Keith opens the front door. His mother's still watching us thoughtfully from the sitting-room doorway, almost as curious about our behaviour as we are about hers.

And everything in the world has changed beyond imagination or recall.

So now we're playing outside, as we've been told.

It's just possible, it seems to me as I look back on it down the corridor of the years, that this was another turning point in the story – that everything thereafter would have followed a quite different course if Keith's mother hadn't made that simple, offhand suggestion – if we'd gone back to his playroom and discussed our shattering discovery there, in the serene and well-ordered world of his official playthings. But outside the house there's only one place where we can talk without being observed or overheard, and once we get there we're across the frontier into another country altogether.

If you know the right spot, in the shrubs that were once the front hedge of Braemar, you can part the screen of vegetation and crawl along a kind of low passageway under the branches into a secret chamber that we've hacked out in the very heart of the thicket. Its floor is bare, hardened earth. A green twilight filters through the leaves. Even when it rains it hardly penetrates this far. When we're in here no one in the world can see us. We've come a long journey from the chocolate spread and the silver picture frames.

Two summers ago this was our camp, where we plotted various expeditions into the African jungle and took refuge from the Royal Canadian Mounted Police. Last summer it was our hide, where we did our birdwatching. Now it's to be the headquarters of a much more serious enterprise.

Keith sits cross-legged on the ground, his elbows on his knees, his head in his hands. I sit cross-legged opposite him, hardly conscious of the twigs sticking into my back or the tiny creatures dangling on threads that catch in my hair and fall down the neck of my shirt. I imagine my mouth's hanging half-open once again as I humbly wait for Keith to announce what we're to think and what we're to do.

I find it very difficult now to reconstruct what I'm feeling – it's so large and complex. Perhaps the *largeness* of the feelings is the most noticeable thing about them. After all the days and years of small fears and boredoms, of small burdens and discontents, importance has come upon us. We've been entrusted with a great task. We have to defend our homeland from its enemies. I understand now that it will involve frightening difficulties and wrenching conflicts of loyalty. I have a profound intimation of the solemnity and sadness of things.

I feel more strongly than ever the honour of my association with Keith. His family have taken on the heroic proportions of characters in a legend – noble father and traitorous mother playing out the never-ending conflict between good and evil, between light and dark. Now Keith himself is charged by fate with taking his place beside them, upholding the honour of the one by punishing the dishonour of the other. And I have been granted a modest foothold of my own in the story, as the loyal squire and sword-bearer that a hero requires.

I think I also understand that he's more than a protagonist in the events we're living through – that he's in some mysterious way their creator. He's done it before, with the murders committed by Mr Gort, for instance, and the building of the transcontinental railway, or the underground passage between our two houses. In each case he uttered the words, and the words became so. He told the story, and the story came to life. Never before, though, has it ever become *real*, not *really* real, in the way that it has this time.

So now I sit gazing at him, waiting for him to announce how we're going to conduct the adventure he's launched us upon. He sits gazing at the ground, deep inside his own thoughts, apparently unaware of my existence. He has moods when he finds me as unnoticeable as his father does.

One of my tasks as his sword-bearer, though, is to prompt his imagination by offering useless suggestions.

'We'd better tell your father.'

No response. I understand why not as soon as I've said the words, and the picture of what they represent comes into my mind. I see us approaching his father as he works in the garden and whistles. We wait for him to look round or draw breath. He does neither. Keith has to raise his voice. 'Daddy, Stephen and I have been reading Mummy's diary . . .'

No. 'Or the police,' I try.

I'm not quite sure, though, what I mean by this in practical terms. I've no experience of reporting things to the police – I've no idea even where you find police when you want them. Police happen when they happen, walking slowly past the shops, cycling slowly up the street. And now, yes, a policeman obligingly comes pedalling up the street inside my head. 'Excuse me,' says Keith politely, while I wait behind him. The policeman stops, and sets a foot to the ground, as he did that day outside Auntie Dee's house. He looks at me and Keith distrustfully, as he did at the children running excitedly up the street beside him then. 'My mother,' he says, 'is . . .'

But the words will not imagine themselves. Not said to a policeman. In any case there's no response from Keith.

My next try: 'We could write an anonymous letter to Mr McAfee.'

Mr McAfee turns into a kind of policeman sometimes, in the evening or at the weekend, though with a flat peaked cap instead of a helmet, and at any rate we know where to find him – at home next door to Keith's house. We wrote him an anonymous letter once before, laying information against Mr. Gort. Keith wrote it himself, in a disguised hand. He addressed it to Mr Mercaffy, and told him that we'd found four human vertebrae. There's no sign so far of Mr Gort's being arrested.

Keith rouses himself from his trance. He feels under the branches at the back of the chamber for the concealed flat stone, and takes out the key we keep underneath it. At one side of the chamber is a dented black tin trunk that we recovered from the rubble of the house, closed with the padlock I was given last birthday for my bicycle. He unlocks it, and puts away the logbook among the other things we keep in there, arranged as neatly as Keith's official toys. There's a piece of twisted grey metal from a shot-down German plane; the stub of a colour pencil, of the sort used by teachers for correcting, that writes blue at one end and red at the other, recovered like the trunk itself from the broken scraps of Miss Durrant's life; a candle stub and a box of matches; four live .22 rounds that Keith swapped at school for a model of a tank; and the Union Jack that we hang from the branches above the trunk to celebrate Empire Day and the King's birthday.

Out of the trunk he takes our most secret and sacred possession – the bayonet with which his father killed the five Germans.

This simple description, though, doesn't do justice to the metaphysical complexity of the object that Keith's now holding. It both is and is not the sacred bayonet, just as the wafer and the wine both are and are not the body and blood of a being who both is and is not a god. In its physical nature it's a long straight carving knife, which we found like so much else in the ruins of Miss Durrant's house. Its bone handle is missing, and Keith has sharpened the blade with the grindstone on his father's workbench so that it has an edge at the back as well as the front, and a point like a rapier. In its inward nature, though, it possesses the identify of the bayonet that goes off with his father to the Secret Service every weekend, with all its sacred attributes.

Keith holds it out towards me. I place my hand on the flat of the blade, tinglingly conscious of the sharpness on either side. He looks straight into my eyes.

'I swear,' he says.

'I swear,' I repeat.

'Never to reveal anything about all this to anyone, except as and when allowed.'

'Never to reveal anything about all this to anyone, except as and when allowed,' I intone solemnly. Not solemnly enough though, evidently, to set Keith's mind completely at rest. He goes on holding out the blade, looking me straight in the eye.

'Allowed by me, Keith Hayward.' – 'By you, Keith Hayward.'

'So help me God, or cut my throat and hope to die.' I recite the words back to him as best I can, my voice subdued by their seriousness.

'Stephen Wheatley,' he concludes. 'Stephen Wheatley,' I agree.

He puts the bayonet carefully down on top of the trunk.

'This will be our lookout,' he announces. 'We'll keep watch on the house from here, and when we see her go out we'll follow her. We'll make a map of everywhere she goes.'

We prepare for the task by clearing discreet windows in the greenery, through which we can see everything that goes on in the Close, and most particularly Keith's house, a little further up on the other side of the street.

A practical difficulty occurs to me. 'What about school?' I ask.

'We'll do it after school.'

'What about when it's tea or supper?'

'We can take turns.'

The time we really need to follow her, of course, is in the darkness at the end of the month, when she goes to her rendezvous.

'What if it's the night?' I ask him. 'We're not allowed to go out when it's night.'

'We'll hide knotted ropes in our rooms. We'll climb out of our bedroom windows and meet here. We'll get some more candles out of the air-raid shelter.'

I shiver. Already I can feel the rough knots of the rope under my hands and the eerie chill of the night air. I can see the candles flickering, and the deep darkness of the night outside. I can hear her soft steps ahead of us as we follow her down towards the shops – past the station – through the bushes above the quarries – out on to the open fairway . . .

'But *then* what are we going to do?' I ask. At some point, it seems to me, there will come a moment when this great programme has to lead to some action by the authorities in the grown-up world.

Keith silently picks up the bayonet and looks at me.

What does he mean? That we're going to arrest her ourselves at bayonet point? Or that we're going to follow his father's example and stick it into the ribs of the courier she's meeting?

Not, presumably, that we're going to . . .? Not his own *mother* . . .!

Keith's eyelids have come down. His face is set and pitiless. He looks like his father. He looks as his father must have looked one grey dawn in the Great War when he fixed his bayonet to the end of his revolver for the battle that lay ahead.

I shiver again. The dark of the moon . . . I can feel it surrounding me, pressing against my eyes . . .

Keith opens the trunk again. He takes out a plain white bathroom tile that we found in the rubble of the house, and the stub of the coloured pencil. With the red end he neatly prints a single word on the tile, and wedges it in the fork of a bush at the entrance to the passageway.

PRIVET, it says.

I don't like to query this, now that he's written it so neatly and authoritatively. In any case, the sense of it is plain enough – that we're commencing a long journey on a lonely road where no one else can follow.

4

She's hunched over a radio transmitter hidden in the cellars of the old castle, tapping on a Morse key, and I'm just about to spring out from behind the secret panel to confront her, when I realise that my name's being called, and I emerge from the shadows of the castle to discover that Mr Pawle is leaning against the blackboard with ironic patience, and that all the class are looking at me and tittering, as they wait for me to answer a question he's asked me; but what the question was, or even what subject we're doing, I have not the faintest idea.

In the lunch hour Hanning and Neale perform their current routine of seizing my ears and rocking my head back and forth as they chant, 'Weeny weedy Wheatley,' and for once I feel sustained against them by the sheer importance of the secret knowledge lodged between those two abused ears of mine.

As soon as I get back from school I run straight to the lookout and start keeping watch on the Haywards' house. But Keith has scarcely joined me before I have to go home for tea, and scarcely have I got back from my tea and he from his before we both have to go home again to do our homework, to eat our supper, to go to bed. It's just as I'd foreseen. We have a task of national importance to perform, and we're endlessly frustrated by all the petty demands of life.

'Fidget, fidget!' says my mother, as I sit at the dining-room table, squirming and sighing over the boiled fish or the Latin translation. 'What's got into you?'

Geoff grins his most maddening sardonic grin. 'Another little game your barmy pal's dreamed up?' he demands. 'What is it this time? Not still after the ape-man on the golf course, are you?'

I endure it all in silence. I should like to drop just the most cryptic hint, and see their faces change. But I don't. I've sworn an oath, and I intend to keep it in the letter and the spirit.

'*Now* where are you off to?' cries my mother, as I wipe my mouth on the back of my hand, or close my exercise book, and jump up to return to my post. 'You're not going to Keith's house again tonight, let me tell you that *right* now.'

'I know, I know – I'm *not* going to Keith's house!'

'No, they're going to be messing around creeping into other people's gardens,' says Geoff.

'You don't know what we do!'

'I've seen you, chum! Hanging around Mr Gort's house, looking for ape-men! It's hell's own pathetic, you know, at your age.'

I've seen *him*, too, hanging around Deirdre Berrill's house. This is too hell's own shameful to bring up, even in an argument.

'Anyway,' says my mother, 'tonight you can just stay in for once. It *is* Friday, after all.'

Yes, it's Friday again, to complicate things still further. It's always said to be *nice* if I stay in on a Friday evening, for some reason, and there's always some kind of unspoken, unexplained reproach hanging in the air if I decline the promise of this niceness and go out.

'Also Daddy's home – he never *sees* you!'

And indeed even my father's home, to cap it all. Dozing in the armchair once again, and beginning to wake at the sound of the argument. He smiles sleepily at me, supporting my mother's case by demonstrating his pleasure at setting eyes on me after so long.

'So,' he says, in his slow, careful way. 'Stephen! Well, well, well! Sit down! Talk to me! Tell me something!'

I sit down reluctantly in the other armchair. Friday – my father – an account of myself demanded. I'm caught.

'Tell you what?' I ask.

'What you did at school today.'

What can I say? Should I tell him about Mr Sankey twisting my right ear, because I couldn't tell him the ablative of *quis*; or about Mr Pawle twisting my left ear, because I was so busy watching Keith's mother transmitting information to the Germans that I didn't even know what it was I couldn't tell him; or about Hanning and Neale distressing both ears simultaneously, because, even after being warned about it so often, I still persist in being weeny, weedy, and Wheatley?

'Revising,' I say.

'Revising what?'

I find it extremely difficult to remember. 'Equations and things. And Canada. In Geography. Wheat and minerals and things.'

'Good,' he says. 'Excellent. So what is the value of x, if $7x^2 = 63$?'

Above his head outside the window hangs a faint cabbalistic sign. It's the pale ghost of the new moon, a back-to-front C written in the clear blue sky like an omen visible only to me. The celestial calendar has begun to mark off the days. First it will swell, then it will dwindle again until it vanishes into blackness. Into x, the unknown in the equation we have to solve.

I've forgotten the terms in the one my father's set me. 'We don't do that sort of equation,' I say impatiently.

'No? Very well, then. What is the approximate value per annum of Canada's output of wheat, in either Canadian dollars or pounds sterling, whichever you prefer?'

I shrug hopelessly. How can I think about the economy of Canada when I know there's a foreign agent somewhere out there in the evening sunshine studying the geography of this very neighbourhood? Marking the co-ordinates of the munitions factory where Mr Pincher works . . . finding secret underground research laboratories in Paradise . . . perhaps bringing off one of the major pieces of espionage that will be recorded with an exclamation mark . . .

My father wants to know everything about my life, now he's got started. On and on he goes, in his mild, careful way. Am I getting on better with the other boys? They're not calling me names any more? This is because I once asked my mother what a sheeny was. She said nothing, but simply propelled me into the dining room, where my father had his work spread out on the table in front of him, and made me repeat the question. I'd realised by this time, of course, that a sheeny must be one of that great class of things that can never be referred to. I'd heard the 'she' in it, and grasped that it was some secret thing to do with girls. My father looked at me for a long time, the way he did when I told him about the Juice at Trewinnick. 'Did someone call you that?' he asked. I quickly shook my head, and felt myself blushing. He went on looking at me. 'Someone at school?' 'No.' 'What else did they say?' 'Nothing.' He sighed, and rubbed his eyes the way he did when he was tired. 'Take no notice,' he said finally. 'Forget it. Sticks and stones, yes? And if anyone ever says anything like that again, you just tell me and I'll talk to the school.'

No, I tell him now – no one's calling me names. So who are my best friends in the class these days? Which is my favourite teacher? Am I enjoying science any more than I used to?

What *I* want to know, though, is why there's something awkward about going out to play on Friday evenings. Why my father has never killed any Germans. Why no one in the whole of the family is in the RAF. Why we have an embarrassing name like Wheatley. Why we can't be called something more like Hayward. There's something sad about our life, and I can't quite put my finger on what it is. Sometimes I come home from school to find I'm kept out of the front room because some melancholy stranger is sitting in it, waiting silently for my father to come home and have an unhappy conversation that Geoff and I aren't allowed to overhear.

It's already getting near bedtime before I can slip away from my unsatisfactory family at last, and rush headlong out of the house. I come out of the gateway so fast that I almost run into her. She's strolling home, back up the Close from wherever she's been. We both stop short, startled once again at the sight of each other, as disconcerted as a big-game hunter and a tiger coming unexpectedly face to face.

'Good heavens, Stephen!' she says. 'Where are *you* off to in such a hurry?'

'Nowhere.' My usual destination, of course, as she immediately realises.

'I'm afraid Keith will be in bed by now, Stephen. Why don't you come and play tomorrow?'

'All right,' I mutter gracelessly, and run back into the gateway as abruptly as I emerged from it.

When I think about this meeting later, after my heart has stopped racing, what strikes me about it is not just her composure, but something else as well. She seemed almost unconscious of the world around her. This is why she was so startled – because she was so busy thinking her own thoughts. And she addressed me direct. I don't think she's ever done that before.

What thoughts was she thinking? I believe I realise, as I recall the look on her face, and the way she called me Stephen, that they were sad ones. I believe it occurs to me for the first time that betraying your country must involve a certain moral anguish, and that there must be even more unanswered questions hanging in the air at the Haywards' house than there are at ours.

I suppose it must be the following Saturday that we get down to serious observation. Peering out from our post through the long empty hours, it's as if we were watching the almost imperceptible current of some dull lowland river, marked only by the occasional passing flotsam or lethargic eddy.

The biggest event of the morning is the arrival of the milk float. First the sounds of its slow approach: the complex ambling of the horse's hooves . . . the faint clink and shift of harness as it waits and moves on . . . Then its appearance in front of us, with the milkman walking behind, absorbed in the familiar worn order book held open by the familiar elastic band . . . Another wait, the horse lost in its own melancholy thoughts, blowing down its nose and copiously urinating as the milkman takes his bottles and tours the next group of houses.

Keith follows him through his birdwatching binoculars as he goes up the path to his mother's kitchen door. Could the milkman be another member of the ring? Spying out the secrets of all the houses he visits – writing them down in the long order book – giving them to Keith's mother to pass on . . .?

'1047 hours,' says Keith, looking at the wristwatch he was given for his birthday, 'milkman arrives.' I write it down in the logbook. '1048 – milkman departs.'

After the milk float has gone Norman Stott emerges from No. 13, carrying a shovel and a clanking bucket. He passes immediately in front of us, talking mournfully to himself, and disappears from our field of view. There's the sound of shovel scraping against gravel. We don't need to see in order to know what he's doing.

'Horse-apples.' This is what my father calls horse manure, for some embarrassing, eccentric reason of his own.

Things look up again for a moment when Mrs McAfee, from No. 8, comes walking slowly down the road, holding something in her hand, and goes into No. 13. This is interesting. The Stotts are not the kind of people that the McAfees would know. Mrs Stott opens the door. They talk . . . Mrs McAfee gives Mrs Stott the thing she's holding . . . Keith peers at them through the binoculars.

'A pair of secateurs,' he whispers.

'Shall I write it down in the logbook?' I whisper. He shakes his head.

Three times an hour there's the muffled sound of a train on the down line as it emerges from the cutting behind the McAfees' house on to the embankment behind the Haywards, rumbles over the tunnel across the lane beyond the Sheldons, and slows for the station. Three times an hour there's the sound of a train on the up line as it slowly gathers speed from the station, rumbles over the tunnel, labours along the rising grade on the embankment, and is swallowed up in the cutting.

The Stotts' dog chases the Hardiments' cat up the street, then, at a loose end, stops in front of the lookout and gazes in at us for a long time, wagging its tail in a puzzled but hopeful way. It's a mongrel with a whitish coat, and a large spot in the middle of its back as prominent as the identification roundel on the wing of a plane. Its attentions must be revealing our presence not only to the entire street but to any passing enemy aircraft.

Eventually it loses interest in us. It yawns and raises its leg at us and goes off to roll in the road. Even the flattened scrapings of horse dung are more interesting than us.

There may be significant things going on at the houses on our side of the street, but we can't see them. On the other side, nothing more happens at Keith's house, after the excitement with the milkman, nothing at the Sheldons or Auntie Dee's, at the Stotts or the McAfees . . .

We note a few developments at Mr Gort's and Trewinnick. Mr Gort comes out of his front door, stands uncertainly in the street for a moment, and goes back inside. At Trewinnick a mysterious hand opens the upstairs curtains behind the evergreens, but we can't see who it belongs to. There's always been something sinister about Mr Gort's house and Trewinnick, of course. But there's something sinister about *all* these silent houses, when you look at them like this. The less you see happening on the outside, the more certain you are that strange things are going on inside . . .

The sun comes out. The sun goes in.

Slowly the strangeness of everything drains away again. A leaden dullness settles over the street. My attention wanders. I pick up the binoculars and look at Keith through them the wrong way round. He snatches them away from me.

'You'll get them out of focus,' he whispers. 'Go home if you're bored, old bean.'

His father's voice, and another of his father's faces.

I don't want to play this game any more, I realise. I squat there on the hard ground under the dull bushes, with the twigs sticking into my back and the caterpillars falling down the neck of my shirt, rebelliously keeping my eyes on the ants hurrying about the dusty ground instead of the stupid nothingness of the street.

I realise I'm tired of pretending to believe all the things Keith tells me. I'm sick of being bossed around all the time.

'Anyway,' I say, 'my father's a German spy, too.'

Keith silently adjusts the binoculars.

'Well, he is,' I say. 'He has secret meetings with people who come to the house. They talk in a foreign language together. It's German. I've heard them.'

This time Keith's lips register a slight dismissive amusement. But it's true! My father *does* shut himself away with mysterious visitors – they *do* talk in a foreign language. I *have* heard them! Why shouldn't it be German? Why shouldn't my father be a German spy if Keith's mother's one, when she doesn't even talk to people in foreign languages – when all she does is make stupid marks in her diary that don't mean anything?

I *will* go home. I start to crawl along the passageway.

'There she is,' he whispers.

I stop and look, in spite of myself. Keith's mother has appeared from the direction of the kitchen door, her shopping basket on her arm. She closes the garden gate carefully behind her, and walks down the road in her usual unhurried way. We both watch, hypnotised. Keith forgets even to look through the binoculars. She passes Trewinnick and Mr Gort's house, and opens Auntie Dee's front gate. She walks up the path, giving a little wave towards the living-room window, opens the front door and vanishes inside.

I pick up the logbook automatically. '1217,' whispers Keith. I write it down. Our boredom has vanished, and all our mutual peevishness and my unbelief along with it.

We stare at Auntie Dee's house, saying nothing. The sense of the strangeness of things returns to me. Why does Keith have an aunt living three doors away? Aunts don't live in the same street as you! They live in remote places to which you go once or twice a year at most, and from which they emerge only at Christmas. And Keith's mother goes to see her not two or three times a year, but *every day*. As I stare at the almond trees and the brown half-timbering of Auntie Dee's house I begin for the first time to see the oddity of the whole relationship. When we go to see Auntie Nora or Auntie Mel we all suffer together. Keith's mother goes to see Auntie Dee on her own. Always on her own. Every day. What do they find to talk about?

I think of the photograph on Keith's mother's desk, and it occurs to me for the first time that if they were sisters when they were little they must be sisters still. An extraordinary thought. It's true that when my mother's talking to my father she sometimes refers to my own Auntie Mel as her sister, but it had never occurred to me to think of grown-up sisters as being sisters in the same way as Deirdre and Barbara Berrill are. I try to imagine Keith's mother and Auntie Dee being jealous and telling tales on each other . . . whispering secrets to each other . . .

What secrets do they have, now that they're grown up? Secrets about Uncle Peter, perhaps. Where he is and what he's doing – little scraps of apparently harmless personal information. But from them Keith's mother will piece together the operations of Bomber Command . . . Even now Auntie Dee may be showing Keith's mother the letter she's just had from Uncle Peter. In it are a few unguarded remarks about how his next leave's been cancelled, and how he's looking forward to bringing the war home to Adolf Hitler personally . . . and when the squadron reaches Berlin on their next mission the Luftwaffe will be mysteriously waiting for them . . . Uncle Peter's plane is the first to be hit . . .

Or could Auntie Dee be a spy as well? Now I see Uncle Peter coming home on leave after all, strolling up the street the way he did before with his cap tipped at a careless angle, and all the children crowding around him. Only this time they're not trying to touch his uniform, they're not asking to be allowed to try his cap on. They're shouting that Auntie Dee has gone – she's been unmasked as a spy, she's in prison. And where's Milly, their baby daughter? She's sitting all alone in their front room, weeping and abandoned . . . I feel a lump coming to my throat, I'm so sorry for Uncle Peter, I'm so sorry for Milly.

Auntie Dee's front door opens, and Keith's mother emerges. Auntie Dee stands watching from the doorstep, unsmiling, her hands pressed to her lips as if she's about to blow a kiss, while Keith's mother lets herself out of the gate and walks away down the street towards the corner with her basket. She's going to the shops once again to do Auntie Dee's shopping for her.

'Time?' I whisper urgently, picking up the logbook, as Auntie Dee shuts the front door again, her kiss still unblown.

But Keith's already scrambling hurriedly away through the passageway, the logbook forgotten. I struggle after him as fast as I can. We're going to follow his mother to the shops.

By the time we emerge from the bushes she's already gone round the corner of the Hardiments' house into the street beyond. We run to the corner after her, and look cautiously round the end of the Hardiments' hedge.

She's vanished.

There's only one way to go when you get to the end of the Close, and that's left, because if you go right the roadway peters out almost at once into a rough track that disappears through the undergrowth into the dark and disused tunnel over which the trains rumble so ominously. To the left, though, is the Avenue lined with little flowering cherry trees that leads long and straight to the main road beyond and the shops where Keith's mother is going.

The Avenue is a different kind of street altogether from the Close. The houses look superficially similar, but as soon as you turn the corner you know you're stepping into alien territory, the beginning of the outside world. Within a few yards of the corner you run up against the War Effort – a smelly mess around the pig bins where the neighbourhood's food scraps are collected. At the far end, on the corner of the main road, is the letter box where Keith's mother posts all that endless flow of suspect correspondence. Just out of sight beyond the corner is the parade of shops that she visits so often and the bus stop where I wait for the 419 to school. There is Paradise – the station where my father catches his train each morning – the munitions factory where Mr Pincher does his pinching – the golf course where German planes land in the darkness . . .

The Avenue stretches in front of us now, clear and straight from the pig bins at this end to the letter box at the other. Hucknall's boy is delivering to a house halfway along on the right. On the left-hand pavement two boys I half know from the bus queue are teasing a small white puppy – the kind of behaviour you'd expect from round-the-corner children. But of Keith's mother there's not a trace. She's walked all the way to the main road in less time than it took us to run half the length of the Close.

We run stupidly after her. By the time we get to the far corner we're both out of breath. We hide behind the letter box and look left towards the parade of shops. Bicycle, prams, people. Two old ladies just getting off a 419 at the bus stop, and three children with swimming costumes getting on . . . My eyes flicker back and forth, struggling to find the one familiar detail we're looking for . . . I can't see it. We look across the main road, up the rutted cart track that leads to Paradise . . . Nothing. We slide round to the left of the letter box and look right towards the station and the golf course . . . No.

She must be in one of the shops already. 'You look in all the shops on this side,' orders Keith. 'I'll do the ones on the other side. Don't let her see you.'

I run from one familiar doorway to another. Court's Bakery, with a scent of warm glazed buns that makes me instantly hungry . . . but no sign of Keith's mother. Coppards, with another delicious familiar smell, of books and pencils, of sweets and newspapers. Mrs Hardiment's in there, looking through the novels in the little circulating library. But not Keith's mother . . . A queue outside the greengrocer's. I don't know how I'm going to stop her seeing me, if she's standing in it and she suddenly turns round . . . But she's not. Another queue in Hucknalls, of course . . . but she's not in that one, either . . . Wainwrights, where I go with Keith sometimes to help lug home bags of chickenfeed . . . Difficult to see past the open sacks of grain and meal piled on the pavement into the poky, sour-smelling darkness within, but I don't think she's there . . .

She's not in the chemist's or the draper's, either, or any of the other shops on Keith's side. She's completely disappeared. We walk slowly back along the Avenue, trying to make sense of it. The shopping basket was a camouflage, explains Keith. She was going to one of her rendezvous. But where?

'It must be in one of these houses in the Avenue,' I suggest. It seems logical, but when you look at them you realise at once that the people who live here are not the kind of people that Keith's parents know. It's difficult to imagine Keith's mother actually walking up to any of these front doors, even for the most pressing and sinister reasons. Keith doesn't comment on the suggestion. 'That manhole . . .' he murmurs, as we pass the studded metal cover near the pig bins. This seems more probable, certainly. It could be the entrance to one of the secret passageways with which the district is riddled. In which case she might be almost anywhere by now – on the golf course, in the old quarry, or at some remote house in the country with shuttered windows and patrolling dogs . . .

Her actual whereabouts, when we discover them a moment later, are more prosaic. And more surprising.

She's at Auntie Dee's house.

The front door opens as we pass, and Keith's mother emerges, her shopping basket on her arm. I feel the same kind of shiver pass through me that I felt when we found the code in her diary. It's not possible! She jumped to the shops before we could get to the end of the Close, and jumped almost instantly back again. Or else we've jumped back in time, and the last fifteen minutes or so haven't existed after all. Once again Auntie Dee stands watching from the doorstep. Once again, Keith's mother lets herself out of the gate. This time, though, she turns not towards the shops but home, then stops as she catches sight of Keith and me.

'So what have you two been up to all morning?' she says, walking companionably up the street with us, while Auntie Dee waves to us and closes the door.

'Playing,' says Keith. I can hear he's as shaken as I am.

His mother, too, realises there's something amiss. She glances at us sharply.

'Oh dear – more funny looks,' she says. 'Something mysterious going on? Something I'm not supposed to know about?'

We say nothing. I suppose we could simply ask her where she's been, but I don't think it occurs to either of us. The world has become one of those dreams where you feel you've lived it all before. Unless the sight of her emerging from Auntie Dee's house fifteen minutes earlier was just something we made up inside our heads . . .

'Anyway, chaps,' she says, 'whatever you're up to I'm afraid you'll have to give it a rest now because it's almost lunchtime.'

Which would be more alarming – to be living in a dream, or in a story that had taken over our memories?

We discuss the problem backwards and forwards as we sit in the lookout over the days that follow, waiting to try again. It's possible that the secret passage under the manhole has a branch leading back to Auntie Dee's house. Or there may be a way in which she could squeeze along the bottom of the Hardiments' garden, which runs alongside the Avenue, then along the bottom of our garden and the Pinchers' – and emerge back into the street by way of Braemar, once she's lured us away from it.

We prise up the manhole cover. There *is* a secret passage down there, but it has an insupportably foul smell, and it appears to be only a foot or two wide. We find a loose board in the fence at the bottom of the Hardiments' garden, but when we force it back the gap's still too narrow for either of us to squeeze through, and in any case there's a stack of glass cloches propped up on the other side.

There seems to be nothing to do but to watch and wait until she goes out again.

What do we see from our vantage point in the meantime? Or dream that we see, or imagine that we see, or imagine later that we remembered seeing?

The policeman, yes. Cycling slowly up the street, appearing and disappearing through the leaves . . . No, the policeman was earlier, before the story began. On the other hand he couldn't have come until Mrs Berrill had seen the intruder . . . Or were there two different policemen, one earlier and one later, who have got run together in my memory?

What I see now through the greenery is Uncle Peter, home on leave, standing outside his house, with his blue uniform flecked with pink by the soft pink snowfall from the almond trees, smiling and happy, surrounded by all the children of the Close. They gape at him, suddenly tongue-tied, their worshipping faces reflected in each of the shining brass buttons on his uniform. The eagle on his hat lifts its proud head beneath the gold and scarlet crown, and spreads its gilt wings protectively over Norman and poor little Eddie, over the Geest twins, over Roger Hardiment and Elizabeth Hardiment, over the two Avery boys and the two Berrill girls, even over my brother Geoff . . .

No, *this* was earlier, too. It must have been, if the almond was in blossom. Keith and I aren't watching from our hiding place – we're there among all the others, transfigured like them by the golden light from the buttons, proud beneath the haughty stare of the eagle . . .

Unless we never saw him at all, and he's stepped out of the black-and-white photograph in that silver frame on the Haywards' mantelpiece . . . But what I remember, as vividly as I remember anything in my long life, are the *colours*! The blue of the uniform, the pink of the blossom, the two spots of blood-red velvet in the crown above the eagle. And I remember the sounds! Of his laughter – of Milly's laughter. He and Milly were laughing because he was holding her in his arms, and she was reaching out to take hold of the pretty gold embroidery on his hat . . .

And now it's night, and the sky's a flickering orange, and there are men in steel helmets running among the tangle of hoses in the street . . . But this was looking out from behind my father in the gateway of our house, much earlier still, when Miss Durrant's house still had a well-trimmed hedge in front of it . . .

What I do finally see from our lookout, though, what I certainly see, is Keith's mother again.

I'm on my own. I think Keith has had to stay at home and help his father build a new extension to the hen house. But suddenly there she is, closing the garden gate carefully behind her, and walking down the road exactly as she did before, unhurried and composed. Past Trewinnick and Mr Gort's house . . . and into Auntie Dee's . . .

I open the logbook. '1700,' I guess, since the watch is with Keith at the hen house. 'Goes into . . .'

But already she's out again. She's closing Auntie Dee's front door behind her, and coming down the garden path, holding not a shopping basket but a letter. She's going to the post for Auntie Dee.

I scramble through the passageway, my limbs muddled with excitement. I'm going to be the one who solves the mystery!

By the time I get free of the bushes she's once again turned the corner by the Hardiments and gone. I run to the corner after her, faster than I've ever run before.

Once again the Avenue stretches in front of me, clear and straight and empty, from the pig bins at this end to the letter box at the other.

This time, instead of blindly running down the Avenue after her, I stand still and think. It's taken me no more than what? – ten seconds to reach the corner. She can't have got to the letter box in ten seconds, even if she'd run all the way. I don't even believe she could have opened the manhole cover, either, certainly not got inside and closed it above her. She couldn't have squeezed through the gap in the Hardiments' fence.

She *must* be in one of the houses – there's nowhere else. Again I try to think clearly. I've run from the fourth house along the

Close, so she can't have got much further than four houses along the Avenue. I walk slowly past the first half-dozen houses on either side, and look carefully at each of them in turn. I don't know what I'm hoping to see. A glimpse of her through one of the windows, perhaps . . . a face somewhere keeping a lookout . . . a short-wave radio antenna concealed behind a chimney . . .

Nothing. Everyone of them is invested with the same undifferentiated, brooding, sinister ordinariness. She could be in any of them.

Again I think carefully. Whichever of them she's in, sooner or later she'll have to come out. All I need to do is wait out of sight, and watch.

I slowly retire to the corner of the Close – walking backwards so that none of the houses in the Avenue is out of my sight for an instant. Even if I have to stay here until bedtime I'm going to make absolutely sure that she can't get back into Auntie Dee's house unobserved again, and emerge like a hallucination as she did before.

As I edge backwards around the corner by the Hardiments some strange presentiment makes me turn and glance briefly up the Close. And there she is – a hallucination already, standing on the doorstep of Auntie Dee's house, half turned to leave, talking to Auntie Dee in the doorway. Once again Auntie Dee stands watching as once again Keith's mother lets herself out of the gate.

Once again I feel the earth shift under my feet.

I stand stupefied as she walks back up the Close towards her house. It occurs to me that she's no longer holding the letter. She's not only jumped back in time – she's jumped forward in space to the letter box first.

Perhaps it's not a spy story we've woven ourselves into, after all. It's a ghost story.

The next time it happens Keith's with me, and we're watching his house so intently that we see her as soon as she comes out of the front door. Keith's father is working in the front garden. She stops to say something to him, then comes out of the gate, carefully closes it behind her, and walks down the street, her shopping basket on her arm once again, as unhurried and composed as ever.

She goes into Auntie Dee's house. We wait, crouched and tense, ready to move. This time we're going to be out of here even before she's round the corner. We're going to be at the corner ourselves before she has time to reach even the manhole cover.

'She could have some kind of rocket thing,' I whisper.

Keith says nothing. I've told him all my theories several times already. Also, he doesn't like the fact that I had the latest mysterious experience when he wasn't there.

We wait. My knees ache from crouching. I try to shift my weight from one leg to the other.

'Or a kind of time machine,' I suggest uneasily, for the fifth time.

Keith's eyelids come down. I understand. If theories involving secret passages, rockets, time travel, and the like are to carry conviction, they have to be uttered in his voice, not mine.

And now there she is, coming out of Auntie Dee's with the shopping basket. At once we're scrambling along the passageway, the twigs tearing at our faces, my hands trampled by Keith's sandals scrabbling the earth in front of me . . . We're out on the street, moving with unbelievable quietness not twenty paces behind her as she walks to the corner . . .

She hasn't heard us. We're round the corner behind her almost without losing her from sight for an instant . . .

And there she is still, walking away from us, just passing the pig bins. We stop and watch her, not daring to move any further, not daring to breathe or to blink. We're going to see the trick done in front of our eyes.

She walks on, still unhurried, still composed. On and on. Growing slowly smaller and smaller . . .

Past the letter box at the end . . . round the corner . . .

To the shops, like anyone else.

* * *

Days go by, and nothing more happens. There's just school, and school, and school, and fights with Geoff, and odd tedious hours of fruitless watching.

One evening we catch her coming out with letters in her hand. She walks down the road, and passes Auntie Dee's without going in. We run to the corner . . . then watch her walk slowly to the letter box at the end and post them. Another day – it must be Saturday – we see her set out with her shopping basket, call at Auntie Dee's . . . and emerge accompanied by Auntie Dee, with Milly in her pushchair. We run to the corner . . . and there they are, dwindling unremarkably away down the Avenue together.

Once we even follow her to the shops. We watch her queuing outside the greengrocer's, catch glimpses of her in the bakery and the draper's, and follow her back to the Close. There's no sign of any rocket or time machine.

It rains, and Keith's mother won't let him go out. It stops raining, and we sit reluctantly under the wet branches of the lookout, yawning and bickering. I know Keith has ceased to believe my account of the second disappearance, although he doesn't say so. I've begun to doubt it myself. Even the first disappearance, that we both witnessed, has drifted back into that realm of the past where inexplicable things no long seem surprising, or in any urgent need of an explanation. We're beginning to take it as much for granted as we do the bush that burned but was not consumed, or the miracle of the loaves and the fishes.

The x's and exclamation marks, too, have receded into the mists. They've become mere runes in an archaic text. The whole concept of night, as the double summer time of the war years takes sunset further and further beyond when we have to go to bed, now seems as remote as the Dark Ages, and the phases of the moon as academic as scot and lot.

Worst of all, we suddenly find ourselves on the defensive. Two brown eyes and a big mocking smile peer in at us one evening through the leaves of the lookout. It's Barbara Berrill. 'You two are always playing in here,' she says. 'Is this your camp?'

I glance at Keith. His eyelids come down, and for a moment he makes one of his father's faces of distaste. He says nothing. He hardly speaks to any of the other children in the Close, never to girls, and certainly not to Barbara Berrill. I feel my own eyelids descend a little. I say nothing, either. I'm stung by her humiliating suggestion that we're merely 'playing' in a 'camp' rather than keeping watch in a lookout.

'What game is it?' she asks. 'Are you spying on someone?'

Keith says nothing. I say nothing, either, but my heart sinks. Our shield of invisibility has been breached, our hidden purposes discovered. And by Barbara Berrill, of all people. She thinks she's superior to us just because she's a year older, but she's not, she's beneath our notice. Everything about her is soft and girlish. Her big brown eyes, her round face, her helmet of pudding-basin hair that comes curling forward on her cheeks. Her school frock, with its blue-and-white summer checks, and its little puffy summer sleeves. Her little white summer socks. Most girlish and irritating of all, for some reason, is the purse slung around her neck, in which she takes her bus and milk money to school each day. She's wearing it now. Why? Keith and I aren't wearing our school caps or satchels. Why are girls like this?

'Who is it?' she demands. 'Not Mr Gort still?'

She's a fine one to talk about spying, when she's spying herself. And how does she know about Mr Gort? She must have been spying on us for ages.

'Go on,' she begs. 'I won't tell anyone.'

We sit it out in silence, our eyes on the ground.

'If you don't say anything, that means you *are* spying . . . Right, then, I'm going to tell on you.'

The brown eyes vanish. 'Keith Hayward and Stephen Wheatley are spying on people!' she says loudly. It's impossible to know whether she has an audience for this announcement or not. She says it again, further along the street. We sit frozen with shame, looking anywhere but at each other. I know now that the whole thing – the disappearances, the secret marks in the diary, everything – was just one of our pretend games. Even Keith knows it. There's nothing we can do but come out of hiding and creep home.

We know without discussing it, though, that we *can't* come out until we're sure that Barbara Berrill's not around to see our humiliation. So we wait. And go on waiting because we can still hear her down the end of the street, laughing with the Avery boys. About us, probably.

The shadows grow longer. I'm going to get a terrible telling-off if I'm not home before eight. Keith's going to get caned.

We sit, heads down, listening. There's a sound of soft, hurrying footsteps. We look up; Barbara Berrill's coming back.

But it's not her. It's Keith's mother. She has her arms folded and a cardigan thrown round her shoulders – and she's hurrying, hurrying down the road into the evening sunlight. She hurries up the path to Auntie Dee's front door, hurries back again almost immediately, and hurries on to the corner. By the time we've collected ourselves and reached the corner as well . . . the street beyond stretches away through the golden air, empty all the way to the letter box at the end.

The hunt's on again.

Only now we don't know where there's left to look or what there's left to try. We run to the manhole and the loose board in the fence. We look hopelessly into houses and gardens.

Nowhere can we find the slightest clue to where she might have gone.

We whisper together, excited again, but more and more uneasy, more and more completely lost. We can both feel the evening getting later and later. In the end we simply have to head for home. I know what's going to happen, of course. She's going to emerge from Auntie Dee's once again as we reach the Close, just as if we'd jumped back to the beginning of the evening, and everything was still in front of us.

And with a kind of dreamlike inevitability she does indeed emerge, only this time from a point slightly further back in time and space – out of the Haywards' own house, exactly as she did before, with the cardigan still around her shoulders. Once again the eeriness of it chills my blood.

'What in heaven's name are you playing at, my precious?' she says to Keith. She speaks calmly, but I realise, from the edge in her voice, and the way she keeps impatiently brushing at her hair, and slapping at something on the shoulder of her cardigan as she speaks, that she's really angry with him for once. 'You know the rules. You know when you're supposed to be in. If you behave like a child then Daddy's going to treat you like a child.'

All her overt anger seems to be reserved for her hair and her shoulder. She keeps brushing and slapping, as if she were unconsciously prefiguring the punishment that Keith's going to get from his father. She and Keith turn to go. Neither of them looks at me.

The last thing I see as she goes is her wiping her hands against each other. The brushing of her hair and the slapping at her shoulder were evidently an attempt to get some substance off them. Now it's on her hands, and it seems to be sticky and difficult to be free of.

And suddenly I know what it is. It's not something sticky. It's something *slimy*.

I know something else, too. I know where she's been each time she's disappeared.

I shiver. The little marks in the diary are true. The dark of the moon's coming, and it's going to be more frightening than we thought.

5

Everything is as it was; and everything has changed. The houses sit where they sat, but everything they once said they say no longer. The re-emergent greenwood has been uprooted and paved over. And Stephen Wheatley has become this old man who seems to be me. Yes, the undersized boy with the teapot ears, following his powerful friend open-mouthed and credulous from one project and mystery to the next, has become this undersized pensioner with the teapot ears, treading slowly and warily in the footsteps of his former self, and he has only this one final project and mystery left.

A surprising thought comes to this old man, as he looks at the district now from the perspective of the years: that in those days all this was *new*. These houses, these streets, those shops in the parade on the main road, the letter box at the corner – they'd been on this earth scarcely longer than Stephen himself. The whole district had been assembled like a Potemkin village, just in time for his family to move here, and for Stephen to discover it as his changeless and ancient birthright.

It was an outgrowth of the railway, of the line emerging from the cutting behind the McAfees on to the embankment behind the Haywards – the line that brought me here today. A few rough, potholed roads had been hopefully laid out around the little wooden country station; various small jobbing builders in nearby villages had bought plots and sketched out their crude private fantasies of rural life in raw brickwork and timber. A few young couples had got off the train at the weekends and looked around . . . paid deposits . . . had three-piece suites delivered and planted privet seedlings . . . needed writing paper and curtain tape . . . found shopkeepers opening up in the new Parade who could supply them. A pole was erected to show where the new bus service would stop, a letter box installed to collect the messages sent back by the settlers to the communities they'd left behind. The muddy tracks were adopted and drained, tarred and gravelled, so that the wives could push their high-sprung perambulators to the shops without jolting their babies awake, and the husbands could walk dryshod in their city shoes to the station each morning and dryshod back at night. The raw earth and bare bricks of the building plots were softened by a green screen that grew as Stephen grew, scarcely further ahead of him in life than his elder brother.

And here's what I'm going on to consider as I look at it now: that this sudden new colony hadn't appeared out of empty desert. A space had to be made for it, bit by bit, in the long-established settlements that occupied the ground already. The new plots were carved out of the smallholdings that had supplied the city with vegetables, out of the orchards growing its apples and cherries, and the meadows that had kept its horses in fodder. The new Windermeres and Sorrentos replaced low timber cottages where the agricultural labourers who worked the soil had lived. The straight gravelled streets rationalised the irregular network of little lanes and paths along which the ploughmen had walked to work and the carters had driven their carts.

And beyond the surfaced streets, in the pockets of land left between this new settlement and all the others appearing at the same time around other stations along the various railway lines, the old world continued. You didn't have to go far to find it. On the way to the golf course you passed abandoned quarries and clay pits, where the cottagers had dug the loam to make the bricks in their foundations and chimneys, and cut the chalk for the lime in the mortar that bound them. On the other side of the main road, just behind the shops, was Paradise, the tangle of mucky smallholdings where our neighbours went to buy unrationed eggs, or a rooster for Christmas. Paradise is now the Paradise Riding Stables and Country Pursuits Centre, and the lane up to it is a well-surfaced private drive. In wet weather then the mud was deep enough to suck your boots off. On our side of the main road there must once have been another lane that had been surfaced to form the Avenue, because if you went to the end of the Close and looked right instead of turning left to the shops you could see where it re-emerged, like a stream from a culvert. A few yards from the corner the new gravelled surface petered out – and there beyond it was the old muddy lane, patiently continuing as best it could, disused by this time and half-choked by encroaching undergrowth. The surface stopped because there were no more houses left for it to go to. This was where our settlement ended, its boundary set by the barrier of the railway embankment.

In the embankment, though, like a disused postern in the walls of a medieval city, you could make out a low brick arch, the entrance to a narrow tunnel grudgingly built by the railway company to preserve the old right of way. And through this humble hole the muddy lane crept slyly on, as it always had, to the unreconstructed world beyond.

I walk to the corner of the Close and look to the right. The rest of the lane has now been surfaced as well. The Avenue continues without drawing breath, and passes beneath the railway through a high, wide bridge, with well-maintained pavements on either side of the road. I walk under the bridge along one of them. On the other side the Avenue branches into a maze of Crescents, Walks, and Meads on an estate now beginning to look almost as venerable as the Close itself.

The familiar world has reached out, and sealed the underworld away beneath the well-drained and well-lit surfaces. Light has joined up with light, and the haunted darkness between them has been abolished.

I walk back along the clean grey pavement, under the clean steel bridge, to the corner of the Close. Behind my back I hear the familiar shifting sound of an approaching train on the down line, as it emerges from the cutting behind the McAfees on to the embankment behind the Haywards. The sound changes again as it crosses the bridge . . . and once again I hear the rumbling hollowness of the old brick tunnel as a train went over, and the never-ending returns of the high cries that Keith and Stephen uttered to test the echoes and show they weren't afraid, as they made one of their rare ventures through that long, low darkness.

Once again I glimpse the perils that lay beyond that echoing ordeal, where the old world resumed after the brief interruption of our familiar streets and houses, as indifferent to them as if they'd never been. We called it the Lanes, though there was only one of them, and so narrow that it almost disappeared in summer into the gross greenery of the hedgerows on either side and the shadows of ancient, crooked trees. I see the Cottages, the sly tumbledown hovels lurking behind the undergrowth in a debris of rusty oil drums and broken prams. I hear the barking of the misshapen dogs that rushed out at us as we passed, and I feel the sullen gaze of the raggedy children who watched us from behind their wicket gates. I smell the sour, catty stink of the elders around the collapsed and abandoned farm where you could sometimes glimpse an old tramp holed up, heating a blackened billy over a little fire of sticks . . .

Beyond the abandoned farm was a desolate no man's land half marked out as builder's lots, where colonisation approaching from the next settlement along had been halted for the Duration. Between the line of the railway and the wasteland of the lots, preserved for a few more years by the shifting tides of history, the last pocket of the rural world pursued its ancient, secret life. Each of the rare excursions we made into it was a frightening adventure, a series of ordeals to test our coming manhood.

And the first of the ordeals was the tunnel itself. Once again I hear our uneasy cries drowned by the huge thunder of the train passing overhead. Once again I see the circle of unwelcoming daylight at the end doubled by its reflection in the great lake that collected inside the tunnel after rain. Once again I feel the awkward twist of my body as I turn to edge sideways along the narrow causeway left at the edge of the lake, and simultaneously lean away from the glistening, dripping wetness

73

of the brickwork. Once again I feel the dank touch of the walls on my hair and shoulder, and brush at the foul exudations they've left. Once again I try to wipe the dark-green slime off my hands.

So her disappearances are quite simple to explain. She's tricked us. The letters she sets off with in her hand, or the shopping basket on her arm, are a camouflage. She's turning not left at the end of the Close, towards the letter box and the shops, but right towards the tunnel. She's passing through that gloomy gateway, edging her way between the water underfoot and the water on the walls, just as we sometimes nerve ourselves to do, and she's journeying into the old world beyond, where there are no shops and no letter boxes, and where no one in the Close but Keith and me ever ventures.

What's she doing there?

Keith and I edge round the lake, keeping our backs away from the slime, our ears ringing with the echoes of every scrape of our shoes against an exposed flint, every drop of water falling from the roof of the tunnel. Keith's in front, of course, but I'm in a state of great excitement because this is all my idea. I'm also uneasier than ever about the terrors of the tunnel; although we waited for his mother to retire for her afternoon rest before we set out, I'm certain that we're suddenly going to hear her footsteps echoing behind us. I keep turning to look at the circle of daylight and its reflection that we've come from, waiting to see the advancing silhouette that will cut us off from home, and drive us helplessly on towards the skulking dogs and children in the Lanes.

We emerge back into the humid afternoon at the far end. The track ahead of us disappears into vegetation standing head-high, and the air's heavy with the buzzing of flies and the choking scent of cow parsley. We look around, uncertain where to begin.

'She may have a transmitter hidden here somewhere,' I whisper, feeling some obligation to offer suggestions in support of my original insight. 'Or there may be some kind of secret research laboratory that she's spying on.'

Keith says nothing. He's maintaining an attitude of judicious caution about my proposals, to remind me that he's still leader of this expedition.

'She can't be going very far,' I point out, before he orders us any further into the terrors ahead. 'She always gets back almost at once.'

We brush the flies away from our faces, and try to read some sense into the undifferentiated tangle of mud and greenery. Only one feature seems to have any distinct identity – the brick circle of the tunnel mouth itself, and the retaining walls that flank it.

'She's spying on the trains,' announces Keith.

Of course. It's so obvious now he's said it that I can't imagine why we haven't thought of it before. Even if the dull electric trains that bear my father and so many of the neighbours off to work in the morning and bring them back at night aren't of any great interest to the German High Command, they're not the only traffic on the line. There are sometimes ancient, grimy steam locomotives hauling long lines of goods trucks. We've seen trains of flatcars loaded with shrouded tanks and guns, and lines of fighters perched with folded wings like queues of resting crickets, from which a trained observer might be able to deduce a great deal of valuable strategic intelligence.

'And she comes to this end of the tunnel . . .' I reason slowly, so that Keith can overtake me and resume full control of the operation.

' . . . so that no one sees her. She's probably got some special place to hide.'

We examine the brickwork. The two retaining walls on either side slope upwards with the gradient of the embankment. At the low end of each is a rusty wire fence hung on concrete posts, and a corroded metal sign warning trespassers off. On one side the wire has come adrift from the bottom of the concrete, and you can curl it back. Keith crawls through; I follow him.

The stalks of cow parsley on the other side have been broken, and there are confused footprints in the mud. Someone has certainly been here before us, and recently. Keith looks at me and narrows his eyes. One of his father's looks, but what it means this time is that he was right, as always.

'Perhaps we should go back,' I whisper. Because if this is where she comes, then she'll come again – and it may be any minute now.

Keith says nothing. He follows the footprints and broken stalks back towards the parapet of the retaining wall, where they seem to end.

'We don't want her to see us here . . .' I begin, but Keith's already clambering on to the parapet, and edging up along it towards the top of the tunnel mouth. 'She can't have gone as far as that,' I object. 'She's always back too soon.' He pays no attention. Reluctantly I clamber up on to the parapet and shakily follow him.

The high end of the parapet brings us almost clear of the undergrowth on the embankment. Just ahead of us is the cleared track where the gangers walk, and beyond it the piled ballast. Seen from this close, the sleepers are massive, and the chairs that carry the rails lift them above the level of our heads. There's a warm reek of creosoted wood and spilt train oil.

So she comes up here and observes . . . counts . . . makes notes . . . memories . . . And then somehow manages to get back to the Close before we've returned from the shops. It doesn't really make sense when you think about it.

'She could be gradually assembling something,' whispers Keith. 'Bit by bit. A bomb. She's waiting for a particular train. With something special on it. A new kind of plane.'

And when it comes . . . another exclamation mark will go in the diary.

A faint metallic disturbance becomes audible. It's coming from just in front of our faces. The rails have begun to murmur the news of an approaching train.

We start to retreat down the narrow parapet. But at once we stop. There's another sound below us – the echoing scrape of shoe against stone, the echoing tumble of stone into water. Someone's coming through the tunnel.

It's her, I know. So, from the look on his face, does Keith.

For a moment, we hesitate, unable to decide which is worse – to find ourselves face to face with his mother, or to lie at the feet of a passing train in all its majestic danger. To be embarrassed or to be killed? Or even worse than being killed, to be somehow caught by the police – taken to court – fined forty shillings . . .

Already Keith's back behind the cover of the undergrowth at the edge of the tracks, and I'm a foot behind him.

We lie like terrified worshippers prostrate before a visiting god as the great dusty bogies fill the sky above us. It's on the up line, right next to us, and the passing showers of sparks spray down on our heads. For carriage after carriage the mighty procession goes on. When at last the wall of noise recedes into the cutting, and we lift our heads to look down into the lane . . . yes, it's her. She's bending down by the hole in the wire fence – not climbing through it, but straightening up and walking back towards the tunnel, holding a letter in her hands once again as if she were going to the post.

Whatever she does here, she's already done it.

We wait until the footsteps in the tunnel have died away to silence, and then a little longer until the beating of our hearts has subsided as well. We edge shakily back down the parapet, and I scramble back through the hole in the wire, leading the way for once, longing to be away from here before the police arrive, or Keith's mother returns, or the dogs and raggedy boys from the Cottages come looking for us.

But Keith's not behind me. 'Keith?' I query, trying not to sound as frightened as I am. 'What are you doing? Where are you?'

There's no response. I climb reluctantly back through the hole in the fence.

He's kneeling in the undergrowth beside the low end of the parapet, where the footprints finish, holding back the cow parsley and gazing at something close to the brickwork. 'What?' I demand. He looks up at me; he has his father's face on again. 'What is it?' I say. He silently returns to inspecting what he's found.

Among the coarse stalks of the cow parsley, tucked into a hollow eroded by the rain behind the brickwork of the retaining wall, is a large tin box. It's about four feet long, and dark green but beginning to go rusty. In embossed and chipped letters on the lid is the inscription: 'Gamages of Holborn. The "Home Sportsman" No. 4 Garden Croquet Set.'

We gaze at it, trying to make some sense of it.

'We'd better tell Mr McAfee,' I say finally.

We go on gazing.

'Or your father.'

Keith puts his hand on the lid.

'Don't!' I cry at once. 'Don't touch it!'

He doesn't withdraw his hand. It remains resting lightly on the lid, still undecided whether to explore further or not.

'It might be the stuff for blowing up the train,' I urge. 'Or it could be booby-trapped.'

Keith puts his other hand on the lid as well, and gently eases it up on its hinges.

The box is completely empty. Its golden interior shines back at us like an untenanted reliquary.

No, there's some small object at the bottom. Keith carefully lifts it out: a red packet, with a black cat on the front of it crowning a white oval that frames the words 'Craven A'.

Twenty cigarettes.

Or is it? Keith opens the flap. Twenty cork tips gaze back at us. Keith slides the drawer out. The twenty cork tips have twenty complete cigarettes attached to them. A scrap of ruled paper from an exercise book comes into view. On it is written one single familiar letter:

X.

That single x haunts my dreams.

What is the value of x, I struggle to calculate, over and over again through the long confusions of the night, if x = K's mother[2] . . . ? X the unknown and the x's in Keith's mother's diary elide with x the multiplier, and the value of x becomes even more mysterious if $x = $ K's mother x January x February x March . . .

Keith's mother's x's elide in their turn with the x's that my mother puts on her birthday cards to me. She bends over me in the dream, as she did earlier to kiss me goodnight, and her lips are puckered into the shape of an x. As she draws slowly closer and closer I see that it's not my own mother but Keith's, and that the x she's offering is minus x: the Judas kiss, the kiss of betrayal. And then, as she comes closer and closer, and the kisses multiply themselves, she becomes the black cat on the cigarette packet, and the blackness of the black cat swells terrifyingly into the dark of the moon.

What do we do next, though? I have no idea.

I sit in the lookout next day after school waiting for Keith. He'll know what to do. He'll have a plan. The dark and shifting dreams will resolve themselves into the familiar secret passageways and underground headquarters. He doesn't come, though. Probably he has homework to do, or he has to help his father. But somehow I can't help feeling that it's something to do with his mother. She's bending over him to kiss him goodnight, her brown eyes shining, her lips pursed into an x . . .

I should go and ask if he can come out to play. But then I think uneasily of his mother bending to kiss him, and I feel somehow reluctant to go anywhere near his house. I start to think about how much harder all this is for Keith than for me. He's the one who does actually have to be kissed goodnight by her. He's the one who has to live in the same house as an enemy agent – to do what she tells him, to eat the meals she prepares, to let her put iodine on his cuts and scratches – and to do it all without letting her suspect for a moment that he knows what she is. Every moment of the day is a further test of his strength, a further demonstration of his heroism.

If Keith's not coming, then I suppose I should go through the tunnel again myself. I should look in the box again and see if the cigarettes are still there. If they are, then I should hide by the railway track and wait to see who comes to collect them . . .

Still I continue to crouch under the bushes, though, going through the motions of keeping watch as before, waiting for Keith to come with the bravery for both of us. After those dreams the darkness of the tunnel seems more fearful than ever. I know that I shall emerge to be confronted by x, the unknown, a dark figure with shrouded face, coming towards me out of the greenery of the Lanes . . . Or worse – I shall hear his footsteps echoing behind me in the tunnel . . .

So many things in life seem to be a test of some kind. Ten times a day, if you're a boy and hope to be a man, you're called upon to brace yourself, to make a greater effort, to show courage you don't really possess. Ten times a day you're terrified that once again you're going to reveal your weakness, your cowardliness, your general lack of character and unfitness for man's estate. It's like the War Effort, and the perpetual sense of strain it induces, of guilt for not doing enough towards it. The War Effort hangs over us for the Duration, and both the Duration and the long examination board of childhood will last for ever.

I get the logbook out of the trunk. '1700,' reads the last entry, from several days ago. 'Goes into.' I'll complete this and bring the logbook up to date, at any rate. I'm still looking for the two-colour pencil, though, when I hear the reassuringly familiar sounds of Keith crawling in along the passageway. My heart leaps gratefully. Now things will be all right.

It's not Keith, though.

'I knew you were playing on your own,' says Barbara Berrill. 'I've got a secret way of seeing you in here.'

I'm so taken aback by the outrage she's committing that I can't speak. She sits on the ground with her arms round her knees, smiling her big mocking smile, making herself entirely at home. She's wearing her school frock with the puffy sleeves, and her school purse slung across her chest. The purse is made of bobbly blue leather, and closed with a shiny blue popper. There's something girlishly self-satisfied about the bobbliness of the leather and the shininess of the popper that offends me almost as much as her intrusion.

'No one's allowed in here!' I manage to cry at last. 'Only me and Keith!'

She goes on sitting and smiling. 'You didn't see me watching you, did you?'

'Yes, I did.'

'No, you didn't.'

'Look, strangers can't come in here. This is private.'

'No, it isn't. It's Miss Durrant's garden, and she's dead. Anyone can come in here.'

'Can't you read?' I point to the warning she's just crawled past. She turns round to look. 'What – "privet"?'

'"Private".'

'It says "privet".'

I cringe with shame on Keith's behalf. 'It says "private",' I insist lumpishly.

'No, it doesn't. And it's stupid to go putting up a sign saying it's privet, when anyone can *see* it's privet.'

'*You're* being stupid, saying things that don't mean anything.'

'What – "privet"?' she says. She rests her chin on her knees, and gazes at me. She's just realised that my ignorance goes deeper than a matter of spelling. At once I'm on my guard. 'Privet' *does* mean something, I realise.

'You mean you don't know what privet is?' she says softly.

'Of course I do,' I say scornfully. And I do, just from the way she asked me. Or at any rate I know that it must be one of those things like bosoms and sheenies that ambush you when you least expect it, so that you suddenly find yourself surrounded by jeering enemies who know what they are when you don't. *Privet*, yes . . . At the back of my mind now I have a dim, shameful recollection of something half-heard and half-understood.

'You don't know!' she taunts.

'Yes, I do.'

'What is it, then?'

'I'm not telling you.'

I'm not telling her because my faint recollection has hardened into certainty. I know perfectly well what privets are. They're the secret little sheds they have behind the Cottages in the Lanes – lavatories of some sort, and of some particular disgusting sort that's full of germs, and that I'm not going to get involved in talking about.

She giggles. 'Your face has gone all squidgy,' she says.

I say nothing. 'Squidgy' is a girl's word that I shouldn't condescend to respond to.

'It's because you're telling fibs,' she teases. 'You *don't* know.'

'Look, just go away, will you?'

I glance in the direction of Keith's house. At any moment he's going to come down the garden path . . . cross over the road . . . come crawling along the tunnel . . . and find our private place full of Barbara Berrill in her school purse, with her school skirt tucked primly over her hunched-up knees, and her knickers on display beneath. He won't blame *her*, of course, or even speak to her, any more than his father ever blames me or speaks to me. He'll hold me responsible for her, just as his father holds him responsible for me. He'll catch my eye and smile that little mocking smile of his. I think of the sharpened bayonet, locked away inside the trunk beside me, waiting for Keith to draw it across my throat to punish any breach of my oath of secrecy.

Barbara Berrill somehow follows the bearing of my thoughts. 'What's in that tin box?' she asks.

'Nothing.'

'It's got a padlock on it. Have you got secret things in there?'

I glance in the direction of Keith's house again. She turns to see what I'm looking at, then turns back and smiles that mocking smile of her own, because she's understood what's worrying me. I seem to be trapped between those two smiles – this one so large

82

and unruly, that one so small and discreet, and yet as sharp as the edge of a sharpened blade.

'Don't worry,' she says. 'I'll go away as soon as he comes.'

She continues to sit there, hugging her knees, and looking at me speculatively. But now she's tucked her chin down into the tautened material of the dress, and I can't see whether she's still smiling or not. Below the hem of the dress the fine golden hairs on the brown skin of her legs catch a little of the evening light.

'Is Keith your best friend?' she says softly. 'Your really *really* best friend?'

I say nothing. I'm no more prepared to talk to Barbara Berrill about Keith than I am about bosoms and privets.

'Why do you like him when he's so horrible?'

I go on looking at Keith's house.

'He's so stuck-up. Everyone except you really hates him.'

She's being spiteful just because she knows he doesn't like her. All the same, I can feel the words 'horrible' and 'hates him' taking hold somewhere inside me like germs, in spite of myself, and I know the infection from them will gradually creep through me like the sour dullness of a low fever.

She knows from my silence that she's gone too far. 'Shall I tell you who *my* best friend is?' she says, her voice soft again, trying to make up. 'My really *really* best friend?'

I keep my eyes doggedly fixed on Keith's house. Something's happening there. Someone's coming down the garden path and opening the gate. It's not Keith, though. It's his mother.

'I'll only tell you if you tell me something secret back,' says Barbara Berrill.

Keith's mother walks unhurriedly down the street. No shopping basket, no letters. I know that Barbara Berrill's turned to look at her as well. She disappears into Auntie Dee's house.

'She's always going there,' says Barbara Berrill. 'Funny having your relations living just down the road, and going to see them all the time.'

For some reason the picture of the box that had contained the Gamages croquet set comes into my head – and another one, too, that's been struggling to surface for some time now: the rusting croquet hoops almost lost in the grass on Auntie Dee's back lawn. Yes – Auntie Dee *is* involved in some way.

Keith's mother re-emerges almost at once. The shopping basket is on her arm once again.

Something brushing against my shoulder makes me glance round. It's the curled end of Barbara Berrill's hair. She's crouching next to me, also watching.

'She's always doing Mrs Tracey's shopping for her,' she murmurs.

I watch in growing agony as Keith's mother walks unhurriedly away into the evening sun, towards the end of the street. I should be out there after her, watching from the corner as she enters the tunnel, from the near end of the tunnel as she reaches the far end . . . But how can I, when I'm being watched myself?

'Funny going shopping in the evening, though,' says Barbara Berrill. 'When all the shops are shut.'

'She's a German spy,' I explain.

No, I don't say the words. Do I? They're filling my head, struggling to burst out of me and quench that mocking smile for ever in astonishment. But I don't actually say the words. I don't think I actually say them.

Barbara Berrill's still looking at me, and she's smiling again. No, I haven't actually said the words. The smile's no longer mocking, though. It's conspiratorial.

'Shall we follow her and see where she goes?' she whispers.

'*Follow* her?' I repeat, shocked to hear my urgent longing articulated for me. 'Don't be daft.'

'Perhaps she's getting something on the black market. From round the back of the shops, like Mrs Sheldon. Deirdre's seen Mrs Sheldon getting things from the back door of Hucknall's after it's closed.'

I'm stung to have Keith's mother's high treason dismissed as such a mean and minor act. 'Of course she isn't,' I say contemptuously.

'How do you know?'

How do I know? Because I know she's not even gone in the direction of the shops! She's beyond the tunnel, bending over the box, putting something in . . . And taking something out, it occurs to me. Putting in another packet of cigarettes . . . and taking out a packet of butter or a few rashers of bacon from one of the Cottages in the Lanes.

Could it all be just that? Going to Coppards for the occasional allotment of the cigarettes that she and Keith's father never smoke, and exchanging them for handfuls of blackmarket groceries? It suddenly seems only too likely. My heart sinks.

I say nothing. I can't look at Barbara. But I can feel her still looking at me, smiling her mocking smile again.

'Or perhaps,' she says softly, 'she's taking a message to Mrs Tracey's boyfriend.'

Now I do turn to look at her, too uncomprehending to conceal it. Auntie Dee's *boyfriend*? What's she talking about? How can someone's aunt have a boyfriend?

'Didn't you know?' whispers Barbara. 'Deirdre's seen her kissing him. In the blackout. She went up to the tunnel with your brother, and there they were.'

I've been ambushed once again. I'm in the middle of another minefield.

'He used to come round to Mrs Tracey's house when everyone was asleep,' says Barbara. 'Only Mrs Hardiment saw him and she thought he was a peeping Tom and she called the police.'

And the policeman came cycling slowly up the street and set his foot to the ground outside Auntie Dee's . . .

'And they told everyone it was because there was something wrong with Mrs Tracey's blackout,' says Barbara. 'But it wasn't, it was because of the peeping Tom – only he *wasn't* a peeping Tom, because Deirdre saw him going into the house loads of times. So instead Mrs Hayward has to go and look after Milly while Mrs Tracey goes out in the dark when no one can see, only now it gets dark too late.'

I can feel Barbara Berrill looking at me to see how I respond to all these revelations. I don't respond. Some instinct tells me that it's just the kind of thing that girls say, particularly the Berrill girls, who are running wild while their father's away. The silver-framed photograph of Auntie Dee and Uncle Peter with the wings on his breast pocket comes into my mind. As soon as it touches the solidity of that silver frame, Barbara Berrill's story bursts like a soap bubble in my hand, and leaves nothing behind but a faint sliminess on my fingers.

'Your face has gone all squidgy again,' she says. 'Didn't you know about people having boyfriends and girlfriends?'

'Of course I did.'

She laughs, her face very close to mine. I feel the sliminess on my fingers. An x is a kiss. On the other side of the tunnel Keith's mother is putting a kiss into the hidden box for Auntie Dee's boyfriend Mr X to find . . .

'It's just while Mr Tracey's away in the Air Force. Deirdre says lots of ladies have boyfriends while everyone's Daddies are away.'

'Barbara!' calls Mrs Berrill's voice. 'Where are you? If you're not home in one minute precisely . . .'

Barbara puts her lips next to my ear. '*Mummy*'s got a boyfriend,' she whispers. 'Deirdre found a snap of him in Mummy's bag. He's an air-raid warden.'

'Barbara! I'm not going to tell you twice . . .!'

Barbara begins to crawl away through the passageway, her purse dangling on the ground. She stops and turns back. She hesitates, suddenly shy. 'My really *really* best friend is Rosemary Winters, in Mrs Colley's class at school,' she says. 'But you could be my next-best friend, if you like.'

After she's gone I sit unable to move, disorientated and then disabled by gathering shame. I've betrayed Keith. I've let a stranger into our special place – and Barbara Berrill, of all people. I've failed in my surveillance duties. And I've allowed myself to listen to unworthy insinuations that his mother's getting bacon and butter on the black market – that she's involved in a surreptitious and shameful traffic with bosoms and boyfriends. I've allowed myself to entertain a momentary suspicion that she's not a German spy at all.

And there she is again, coming back up the street from the corner . . . going into Auntie Dee's gate . . . tapping quietly on the living-room window as she passes. The front door opens as she reaches it, and Auntie Dee stands on the doorstep.

Keith's mother hands her the shopping basket. She's done Auntie Dee's shopping for her once again. While all the shops were shut.

Auntie Dee searches through the contents of the basket. She's looking for the message that Keith's mother has brought her back from her boyfriend . . .

Only of course she isn't. I think of her friendly, open smile. No one could smile like that and have any secrets from the world. I think of the trusting way that Uncle Peter smiles back at her from the silver frame on her mantelpiece.

She's not smiling now. She's plucking anxiously at her lip. But she's looking up at Keith's mother, trustingly and apprehensively, just like the little girl with the doll in the other picture who looks up so trustingly and apprehensively at the older sister who will always protect her.

Sisters . . . Yes. What are those two sisters talking about so earnestly there on the doorstep? They're telling each other the kind of things that Deirdre and Barbara tell each other. Secrets . . . About kisses in the blackout . . .

Keith's mother turns and walks back to the gate. She looks exactly as she always has – composed, tranquil, at ease with the world. Auntie Dee stands on the doorstep and watches her go. She's changed in some subtle way. She's become a person with secrets after all.

Auntie Dee closes her front door. A few moments later Keith's mother closes hers. The curtain has come down again.

* * *

'1700. Goes into.'

I'm back at my post next day, logbook open once again, and I'm just hesitating, two-colour pencil in hand, trying to remember what it was that Keith's mother did go into at 1700, when my eye's caught by a movement at the Haywards' house.

Once again the same scene's unrolling. Keith's mother is coming out of her garden gate with her basket on her arm. She's going back to Auntie Dee's to whisper more secrets . . . No, this time she walks straight past Auntie Dee's . . . Not that I believed any of Barbara Berrill's ridiculous stories about them, even for a moment.

She goes on towards the corner, and I know that this time there's no way out of it: I'm going to have to follow her. Through the tunnel. On my own.

How I'm ever going to find the courage I don't know, but already I'm scrambling along the passageway, running down to the corner, turning towards the tunnel . . .

And once again she's vanished.

The track winds through the encroaching undergrowth to the tunnel, as empty as the street to the left was each time she vanished before. I feel the familiar cold wave pass through me.

Then behind me I hear a small, familiar sound – a dry rustling and a wet slithering. I spin round. There she is, just beyond the corner to the left, tipping food scraps out of an old newspaper into the pig bins, and watching me thoughtfully. She lets the lid clank back into place, and smiles. 'Hello, Stephen. Are you looking for Keith?'

Left, yes. There's still left as well as right. And the pig bins. Of course.

I shake my head stupidly.

'You seem to be looking for *somebody*.'

'No.'

'Not *me*, was it, Stephen, by any chance?'

'No, no.'

I flee, and hide my confusion under the bushes. As she passes on her way back to the house she turns and looks in my direction. I don't know how she realises I'm there watching her, when it's supposed to be secret, but she does; and when she emerges from the house again ten minutes later I know that this time I'm really not going to have the courage to follow her.

She's not carrying a basket, though; she's holding a plate. And she's not walking down the road towards Auntie Dee's house or the corner. She's crossing over . . . and coming straight towards me. I sit absolutely motionless as she peers in through the branches. 'Stephen?' she murmurs. 'May I come in?'

I can't manage a reply. In all the places that we've imagined her going, and all the contingencies that we've dimly foreseen, we've never considered the possibility of her coming *here*.

I'm too embarrassed to watch her as she struggles in along the low passageway. I know she has to make an awkward spectacle of herself, encumbered by the plate and leaning her weight on her other hand to keep her knees just clear of the earth, so that her back's too high, and the twigs keep catching at her cardigan. She brushes a patch of ground as clean as she can of leaves and insects, then sits down cross-legged in the dust in front of me.

I don't know what to do with myself. It's difficult enough to know how to behave when you're on your own with someone's mother, even in the most normal of circumstances. But what do you do when you're both sitting childishly on the bare earth, face to face in a space scarcely large enough for people half her height?

And when you know that she's not just someone's mother – that she's a German spy, a traitor to her country?

Where do you look, for a start, when there's nowhere to look except at her? You can't look her in the face. You can't look at her legs, neatly but somehow shamefully crossed beneath her navy-blue summer skirt. There's nowhere left except the bit in between, and that part of a lady, as I've known for a least a year now, is her bosom, and as unthinkable-about as a privet.

She puts the plate down in the small space between us. It's decorated with roses, and there are two chocolate biscuits on it.

'I thought you might like something to keep you going,' she says. 'I'm afraid Keith's got to help his father in his workshop, so you're going to have to play on your own this evening.'

I pick up one of the biscuits and nibble it, grateful to have something to do and some object to look at. Silence. Can she have come all the way across the road, and seated herself cross-legged in the dust in front of me, just to tell me that?

But she seems to be looking round at our domestic arrangements, like any polite visitor on a social call.

'Very thoughtful of you chaps to put that label on it,' she says, indicating the tile guarding the entrance passageway. ' "Privet".'

At the sound of this impropriety on her lips, I feel my face getting into the same awkward state that Barbara Berrill commented on in such embarrassing terms. Perhaps she doesn't know what the word means. I try not to look at her bosom.

'Awful smell it's got in summer,' she says. No, she does know. 'But what a lovely hidey-hole it makes!'

She picks up the open logbook. I remember the list of dates, with all the x's and exclamation marks, and my muscles freeze with my polite mouthful of chocolate biscuit half-swallowed in my throat.

She closes it, though, and looks at the inscription on the cover: LOGBOOK – SECRIT. She laughs. 'Oh dear. That's Keith's handiwork, is it?'

I want to lie and say it was me, to spare Keith's shame, but no words emerge through the biscuit. I want to snatch the book away from her before she opens it again, but no movement issues from my hands.

She looks back at the sign over the passageway and laughs again. 'Oh, I *see*!' she says, '*Private*! How priceless!'

She puts the logbook down. 'I suppose I'd better not look inside if everything in here's so terribly hush-hush.'

I swallow the crumbs of chocolate biscuit. She looks out through the branches.

'It's a frightfully good place for a lookout, though,' she murmurs. 'You can see everything that goes on in the street. That's what you're up to in here, is it? Keeping watch on us all, and writing it all down in your logbook?'

I still can't answer. Simple words like 'yes' and 'no' seem to be superimposed upon my tongue so that they cancel each other out.

'I think Keith's got some binoculars somewhere that he uses for birdwatching. They might come in handy.'

Yes/no. Already using them/nothing to use them for.

'So what have you seen so far? Anything terribly suspicious?'

My head shakes itself. Perhaps I'm beginning to recover from my first shock. But in the silence that follows, as I go on trying not to look at her bosom, I can feel her smiling encouragingly down at the top of my head, and then her smile becoming serious. There's more to come.

'Well, I hope the Mounties get their man and all that, and I certainly don't want to spoil your game. You chaps might just keep in mind, though, that even the best of games can sometimes get a bit out of hand. It would be a terrible shame if you upset any of the neighbours. For instance, I think it might be perhaps just a *tiny* bit rude if you actually followed people around.'

So she's seen us. In which case, why isn't she telling Keith off rather than me? Everyone knows you tell your own child off, not somebody else's, for offences they've committed together. Why has she come all the way across the road to say it to *me*, when Keith's not here?

'It's such fun for Keith,' she says, 'finding a real friend, because it does get a bit lonely sometimes if you don't have any brothers or sisters, and he doesn't make friends easily. I know you've got lively imaginations, the pair of you, and I know you have tremendous adventures together. But Keith's easily led, as I'm sure you realise.'

I look her full in the face for the first time in sheer astonishment. Does she *really* not know that Keith's the instigator and commander of every enterprise we undertake? Can an experienced espionage agent have really so completely misunderstood what she's observed? I suppose it's yet another tribute to Keith – he's obviously as good as his parents are at concealing his true nature from everyone around him.

Her eyes are brown, like Barbara's, and they've lost the calm complacency with which she's always regarded me in the past. They're bent on me as intently as Barbara's were while she watched me to see if I was shocked by her stupid stories. The light in Keith's mother's eyes, though, isn't teasing. She's entirely serious.

'I don't want to have to stop him seeing you,' she says, very softly. 'But then I don't want him getting into any kind of trouble.'

Her voice becomes even softer. So do her eyes. Now that I've looked into them I can't look away. 'Sometimes people have things they want to do in private,' she says. 'Just like you and Keith in here. They have things they don't want everyone talking about.'

I have a sudden fear, as she goes on looking at me and I go on looking at her, that she's going to confess everything. I want to beg her not to. I don't want to hear it. I don't want to have to know for sure.

But she glances away. 'Silly little things, perhaps,' she says. 'I don't know . . . Well, Mr Gort, let's say. If he decided to go out to the Railway Tavern one evening and have a glass of beer, he might prefer not to have people watching him and then going around announcing to everyone "Oh, Mr Gort's in the pub again." Or Mr and Mrs Stott. I don't suppose they like people following poor Eddie about and staring at him. Or say you started trailing round after the people at Trewinnick. It might make them feel a bit self-conscious about their appearance.'

Her examples are unconvincing. Everyone knows Mr Gort goes to the pub. Everyone knows you're not supposed to stare at Eddie Stott. And surely it would be a good thing, not a bad thing, if the Juice at Trewinnick became aware of how alien we found them. So she's not going to say who it is she really doesn't want us following, or why. She's not going to confess. I'm half relieved and half disappointed.

'Anyway,' she says, picking up the empty plate. 'I know you're a sensible, well-brought-up boy, and I thought I'd have a quiet word with you on your own, while Keith's not here. And we'll keep this between ourselves, shall we? Probably best not to say anything to Keith about our little chat.'

I nod. What else can I do?

'So you see I'm trusting you. I'm putting you on your honour. Yes?'

I nod helplessly once more.

She puts her hand on my arm and looks straight into my face. 'You won't let me down, will you, Stephen?'

I shake my head. She goes on gently holding my arm and looking into my face. Then, with a kind of little sigh, she lets me go, and begins to clamber back along the passageway. She stops and looks at the PRIVET sign. 'I'm terribly sorry about that,' she says. 'So silly of me not to guess. I promise I won't intrude again.'

She struggles on a little further, then stops and turns round once more.

'You haven't been to play at the house for ages,' she says. 'Why don't I tell Keith to ask you to tea tomorrow?'

I try to take stock of the situation, as she disappears back into the outside world. Once again I've let strangers into our private place. Once again everything has changed.

After she's gone I remember the back of her dress as she clambered awkwardly away from me along the passageway, its calm simplicity confused by the dust of the bare earth, its elegant regularity mocked by the random detritus of dead leaves and twigs hanging from it. And I feel somehow . . . sorry for her, in spite of her crimes. I feel pained that she's had to humiliate herself before me in this way.

I jump out of my skin, because I've just realised that she's peering in at me through the branches again. She's no longer holding the plate. Once again she has her shopping basket on her arm. She's smiling. Her brown eyes are calm once more.

'Thank you for having me,' she says.

She walks calmly down the street towards the corner.

I watch her go. This time, of course, she *is* going through the tunnel.

I make no move to follow.

6

What is it that wakes me? Is it all my anxieties about the task we've taken on, and about what to do now that Keith's mother has told me to abandon it? Or is it my bad conscience about all the weakness I've shown and all the wrong thoughts I've allowed myself to think?

Or is it merely the unnatural lightness of my blacked-out bedroom?

There's a strange white light flooding around the edges of the blackout. I get up and slip my head under the blind. The dull, familiar world outside, I discover, has been transformed. The tangle of bushes in our front garden and the frontages of the houses opposite are picked out, against a background of velvet darkness, in the most delicately brilliant and unearthly white. There's absolute stillness, absolute silence. It's as if the Close had become a picture of itself, or as if the ethereal chiming of the Haywards' clocks had been caught and preserved as a silent shape in space.

Night – the almost forgotten time. And the full moon, pouring softly down from somewhere above the roof of the house, smoothing out all the muddle of the garden and the blemishes of weathered render on the houses opposite, washing away all the shame and confusion of the day, leaving only this perfect white stillness.

We're halfway through the lunar calendar. Halfway to the next dark of the moon.

And what am I going to do? I plainly can't go on watching her and following her now she's seen us doing it and put me on my honour to stop. But I plainly can't stop watching her and following her now that she's more or less told me that if we go on we may find out something that she doesn't want us to know.

I obviously have to talk to Keith about it and let him work it out. She's his mother! She's his spy! But just as obviously I can't tell Keith about it, because she told me not to. She told me not to and I helplessly nodded my head. I agreed. I as good as gave her my word.

Even before this there were a lot of things piling up that I couldn't tell Keith about. Barbara Berrill's visit. Her stupid stories about his mother and his aunt. Now I've been burdened with another secret that I have to keep from him. But how can we possibly proceed if I don't tell him this one?

I feel as if my head's going to burst with trying to accommodate all these contradictions. But then, as I go on gazing at that serene white world outside the window, everything begins to seem simple after all. If only I had a knotted rope, as Keith had suggested, I should climb out of the window and let myself down into that great calmness. I should take it into me and become part of it. I should perform one simple heroic deed that would settle everything once and for all.

I should go through the tunnel now, while the world's completely still, and she's not there to be watched or followed. I should discover what it was she left in the box this time, before anyone has a chance to remove it. I should find the evidence that would prove beyond all doubt that Keith's right, and that his mother really is a German spy.

One single heroic deed, to lay at Keith's feet in the morning. And with that one blow all my problems would be solved and all my weaknesses and errors wiped away, as surely as all the defects of the day are dissolved by the moonlight.

I should go through the darkness of the tunnel. On my own. And out into the moonlight beyond.

If only I had a knotted rope . . .

The white stillness goes on and on. I've never seen the world like this before.

Slowly it comes to me that I don't actually need a knotted rope. I could simply walk down the stairs.

Now I've thought the thought, I know I have to do it. I know I'm going to do it.

And at once I'm terrified. The summer night has become suddenly freezing. I start to shiver so uncontrollably that I can scarcely get the jumper over my head or the sandals on my feet. I can hear my teeth rattling together like dice in a shaker. Geoff stirs in his sleep, as if he'd heard them too. I feel my way downstairs, and through the kitchen to the back door. Very slowly I ease back the bolt, still shaking. I step silently out into the silver darkness, and become part of it.

Never in my life before have I crept out of the house in the middle of the night. Never before have I experienced this great stillness, or this strange new freedom to go anywhere and do anything.

I shan't have the courage to go through with it, of course. I shall die of fear before I get beyond the end of the street.

I must do it, though, I must.

Between the reflected disc of silver-grey behind me and the second one in front of me is a darkness whose shape is defined entirely by sound. The huge reverberations of the water plopping from the wet blackness overhead into the black water beside me merge into suites of scutterings and splashings trailed by unseen nocturnal creatures fleeing before the long echoes of my panicky breathing. In my terror I lose my footing on the unseen narrow causeway along the edge of the unseen lake, and have to keep touching the slime on the walls to steady myself. The slime is full of germs – I'm getting germs all over my hands.

And then at last I'm out into the open night again, and looking up in gratitude at that serene white face riding full and round above the railway embankment. The night's coming when I shall be out in the darkness again with no moon to whiten the world. And even as I think the thought, a cool breath of air stirs, and the moon sails behind a cloud. The delicate white world around me evaporates.

I stand stock still, mastering my new access of panic. Slowly I piece together a world of sorts from the different densities of blackness around me, and from a few small sounds. The stirring of the leaves in the trees along the lane. The murmur of the telegraph wires along the railway track above me.

I creep forward again. By touch I find the harsh brickwork of the retaining wall . . . the rusty links of the wire fence . . . the broken stalks of the cow parsley . . . the metallic smoothness of the box and its embossed inscription.

I listen. The rustle of the leaves, the murmur of the telegraph wires. My own breath. The distant barking of the dogs at the Cottages in the Lanes. Nothing else.

I ease the lid open. The shiny underside as it turns catches a faint gleam of light from the clouds. There's no trace of any light reflected from the bottom of the box, though. I'm looking into blackness. There's something odd about the blackness – something wrong with the *sound* of it . . . What's wrong is that there *is* no sound. The hard interior surfaces should give back a faint response to the tiny atmospheric breathings of the night, and no response is forthcoming.

I cautiously put my hand inside. The texture of the air seems to change and thicken around my fingers, as they sink into some substance that gives beneath them. I snatch my hand away.

What I felt, I work out with hindsight, as my surprise subsides, was a *softness*. A dry, cool softness. The box has something in it. Slowly I work out what it was.

Some sort of cloth.

I put both hands very slowly and carefully back into the box. Cloth, yes . . . A lot of cloth . . . Different sorts of cloth . . . Some of it smooth, some of it fibrous . . . A hem . . . A button . . . Another button . . .

Underneath my fingers now is something rough to the touch, with a pattern of ridges and furrows that seems curiously recognisable. I think I know what it is. I slowly ease my hand right round it to feel its underside and its width – then stop.

The texture of the darkness around me is changing a little. I look up, and see the suggestion of a luminous edge to the clouds overhead. At any moment the moon's going to come out again.

But something else has changed, too. Something about the *sound* of the world . . .

I strain my ears. Nothing. Just the shifting of the leaves, the sigh of the wires, the coming and going of my breath . . .

I focus my attention back on the object I'm touching. The underside of it feels the same as the top. It's about as wide as my hand . . . Yes, I know what this is. I begin to slide my hand along it, so that I can feel the end of it to check, then stop again.

The sound that's changed, I realise, is the sound of my breathing. It's grown more complex. It no longer corresponds precisely to the rise and fall I can feel inside my chest.

I stop breathing. The sound of breathing continues.

There's someone a few feet away in the lane – someone who has come silently up to the gap in the wire fence and then stopped to listen, as I'm listening now.

Another faint sound. A hand feeling for the brickwork of the retaining wall, just as I felt for it . . . Now the rusty links of the fence are being eased back. A body's squeezing underneath them . . .

There's someone very close behind me, feeling his way towards the box. It's a man – I can hear the maleness of his level breathing. A grown man – I can hear the size of him. In another moment I shall feel his hands as they reach out towards the box and encounter my back instead.

I can't move. I can't breathe. An agonising electric coldness passes through my back as it senses the approach of those hands.

And all at once the darkness dissolves in a flood of moonlight.

The level breathing behind me ends in a sharp, raucous gasp.

Neither of us moves. Neither of us breathes.

I've only to turn and I shall see him. But I can't, any more than you can ever turn when you hear the terrible figure behind you in a nightmare.

Then the moon's behind the clouds again and the man's gone. I hear him scrambling back through the wire fence, and stumbling in his haste as he runs into the rutted depths of the Lanes.

I wait, as immobile as stone, still charged with that unbearable cold electricity.

I wait . . . and wait . . . until I hear the dogs barking in the distance again, and I know for certain he's gone. Then I turn and hurl myself unseeing through the tangle of the fence and into the booming darkness of the tunnel.

The Close, as I come running blindly round the corner, is full of wildly swinging torch beams and demented figures running back and forth. The torches swing at once towards me and stab at my eyes. A storm of frantic clutching and whispering bursts over me.

'Where have you been . . .? What in heaven's name do you think you're doing . . .? Have you gone out of your mind . . .? We were going to call the police . . .? Do you know what time it is . . .?

The streetful of frenzied figures resolves itself into my two parents in their dressing gowns, hustling me towards our front door, still trying to keep their voices down so as not to wake the neighbours. Geoff watches sardonically from the doorstep. I suppose it's Geoff who told on me.

As soon as the front door closes behind us, they're free to raise their voices at last, and when my father turns on the lights a fresh subject for consternation appears. 'You're soaking wet!' cries my mother. 'You're wet from head to foot!'

It's true; I seem to have run straight through the water in the tunnel and fallen headlong.

My mother tears the wet clothes off me, as if I were three years old again.

'Jesus wept,' says Geoff. 'What were you hunting this time? U-boats?'

'Oh, this was some tomfoolery with Keith, was it?' shouts my father. I've never seen him in this state before.

'Keith?' cries my mother. '*Keith*'s not running around out there as well, is he?'

I say nothing. My teeth have started to chatter again.

'*Is* he?' demands my father. 'Have I got to go knocking on his door to check he's home?'

At this transcendentally awful prospect I change my policy and shake my head.

'You're *sure*?' says my mother. 'You're sure you didn't get Keith into this kind of state as well? Because if you did I don't know *what* his mother will be thinking!'

Once again I shake my head. Does she really think that I'm the one who gets Keith into states, and not the other way round? How has Keith managed to fool both our mothers so completely?

'So what were you up to?' demands my father. 'If you wouldn't think it impertinent of me to enquire . . .'

But here I revert to total uncommunicativeness. Am I deliberately refusing to speak about things that I know must never be revealed to outsiders? Or am I simply too shocked to open my mouth? All I can think, as I stand there naked and shivering, mute and infantile, is one single despairing thought: that I could have turned round and seen who it was. I could have turned. I could have seen him. I've failed yet again.

There's something still clutched in my hand, I discover, as my mother throws a towel round me and rubs me violently dry – the ridged and furrowed thing that I took hold of in the box just before I heard him coming. I examine it at last, and it's exactly what I thought it was. It's as sodden as everything else, and my mother snatches it out of my hand and throws it down on the wet heap piled on the floor beside me.

It looks entirely at home in its new surroundings: a long woollen sock, dark blue, with a heavily darned heel.

Keith turns the sock over in his hands, inspecting it carefully. The darn has dried a paler colour than the rest, now I've recovered the sock from my mother's washing basket, and the sole's brown with age and use. He turns it inside out. There's nothing concealed in it except a few little balls of woollen fluff.

We're sitting at the tea table, under the gleaming silver of the candlesticks and the ashtray that this parents won in the world tennis championships. My heart sinks as I watch him. This is the fruit of my great exploit, the treasure that I went out in the night to fetch and lay at his feet. It should be something else, of course. If it had been Keith who had done the deed it would be. It would be a map or a plan of something, perhaps. A message in code. At the very least another packet of cigarettes with a secret sign in it. Not a sock, though. Not an old sock.

On the shining, dark tabletop, under Uncle Peter's straightforward gaze from the mantelpiece, the brown sole and the darned heel stand out with unnatural distinctness.

'There were other things in the box,' I explain once again. 'Shirts and things. I just happened to be holding that. When I heard the man.'

I've told him about the man, and the dogs barking in the Lanes. I haven't told him about the moon coming out. I haven't told him that I could have turned round and seen the man in the moonlight.

Keith's eyelids come down a little; one of his father's looks again. My great exploit hasn't pleased or impressed him. I should have guessed. He's the one who's the hero of our projects, not me.

'And you're sure he didn't see you?' he demands.

'I hid,' I say, not looking at him. 'I hid very quickly.' I realise now – I've done everything wrong.

'And you didn't get a proper look at him?'

'I couldn't. I was hiding.'

Keith turns the sock over again, dissatisfied with either it or my explanation, or both.

'I thought it might be a disguise,' I suggest humbly. 'I thought it might be sort of ordinary clothes for someone to change into. If they'd landed by parachute or something and they were wearing a German uniform. If they were hiding in the Lanes somewhere.'

At any rate an old sock plainly isn't payment for off-the-ration bacon, or a present from Auntie Dee to some imaginary boyfriend. Not that I ever believed those stories for a moment. Or could have said anything about them to Keith even if I had. It would be telling tales. You can't tell tales. Certainly not about someone's own aunt, about someone's own mother.

I snatch the sock off the table and hide it in my lap as his mother comes into the room.

'I don't know whether Stephen likes Chelsea buns?' she says. 'It's all I could get in Courts.'

She smiles at us both collectively with her usual careful imprecision. Everything, she's telling me, is to be as it always was. But it isn't, it isn't! Under the tabletop I'm holding the old sock that she put into the box for X, for a German parachutist, and that I took out again in spite of what she said. I can't look at her. I know my face is in a bad way again. 'Thank you,' I mumble.

She goes out again, but I haven't the heart to put the sock back on the table. 'Why did you take it out of the box?' demands Keith now, still dissatisfied, undistracted by the buns. 'When they find it's missing they'll know someone else has been there.'

I say nothing. I can't explain how I came to find it in my hand afterwards without mentioning my panic-stricken flight, and I can't explain my flight without mentioning the figure breathing behind me, and my shameful failure to turn and look at him.

I choke down my bun in silence.

'We'd better go and see what's happening,' he says. There's a note of conscious forbearance in his voice. He's resuming the burden of leadership by taking upon himself the wearisome responsibility that a leader has to accept for his subordinate's mistakes.

I make a belated effort to honour my agreement with his mother. 'We'd better not,' I say.

Keith's eyelids come down again. 'Why not?' he demands – and of course I can't explain. He thinks I'm frightened. All my bravery in the night now counts for nothing.

'I just think we'd better not,' I repeat feebly.

He leads the way to the sitting-room door and taps on it as usual. 'Me and Stephen are going out to play,' he announces.

There's a pause while she thinks about this. I can see her beyond him, sitting at the desk with the blotter open and a pen in her hand. She's weighing up whether to trust me to keep to our agreement, and to keep Keith to it as well.

'"Stephen and *I*",' she murmurs calmly at last. She's trusting me.

'Stephen and *I*,' he repeats obediently. He steps back. I step forward to take his place and observe the usual ritual.

'Thank you for having me,' I mumble.

She smiles, perhaps at hearing the formula on my own lips again.

'Have fun, then, chaps,' she says. 'Try not to get up to any mischief.'

She's reminding me of our compact, and of course as I trail behind Keith to the end of the street, breaking that compact and letting her down at each step of the way, I feel worse than ever.

At the corner we stop and look cautiously back to check that the street's empty behind us.

'She was writing letters,' says Keith. 'She'll be going out to the post again soon.'

I know. And will be turning right instead of left, and catching us looking in the box, and discovering my betrayal. I follow Keith helplessly through the echoing darkness, between the water and the slime, trying to persuade myself that since we're ahead of her we're not actually following her. We curl back the wire fence and crawl through.

In the vegetation by the retaining wall there's now nothing to be seen but the lingering shape of an indistinct absence. The box has gone.

'He obviously did see you,' says Keith. 'They've moved their hiding place. So now the Germans know we know about them. We've got to start all over again, old bean.'

My heart shrivels at the sound of his father's tone and his father's phrase, at the accusing absence in the undergrowth, at my hopelessness.

'I'm sorry,' I say humbly.

Breaking my word of honour has had nothing but bad consequences. And at any moment she's going to be arriving with her next consignment of secrets to put in the box. She's going to find it gone – and me there as the cause of its disappearance.

'I'm sorry, Keith,' I whisper. 'We'd better go.'

But Keith's smiling his dangerous little smile. I know I'm going to be humiliated for being so hopeless, and for my presumption in trying to demonstrate otherwise.

'So *he* saw *you*,' he says. 'But *you* didn't see *him*.'

I'm choked by the unfairness of this. Keith doesn't know how terrifying it was to be here, on my own, in the middle of the night! He's not the one who experienced it!

'It was dark,' I explain.

'It was moonlight. You said it was moonlight.'

'Not then.'

'When?'

'When he saw me. When I didn't see him.'

The weakness of this answer dawns on me even as I say it. Keith's smile becomes even narrower, his voice even softer.

'You weren't really hiding, were you?' he whispers. 'You were just hiding your face.'

'Keith, please – let's go home.'

'You were just putting your hands over your face. So you couldn't see. Like Milly playing hide-and-seek. Like a little baby.'

I feel the choking obstruction growing in my throat, then the shameful tears beginning to obstruct my vision. It's the sheer unfairness of his accusation that undermines me, his grotesque concentration on my one moment of weakness after I'd demonstrated so much courage, his cruel rejection of the hard-won tribute I'd laid at his feet. But of course my tears are now the proof of his point. Through their wavering wetness I'm conscious of his smile slowly evaporating. He turns aside and shrugs. He's lost interest in me. 'Go on, then,' he says. 'Go home, if that's what you want to do.'

I crawl back to the gap in the wire fence, still whimpering, more humiliated than I've ever been. I struggle to push the wire aside, and in my distress I fail even in this.

Then I stop. I try to suppress my sobs while I listen.

From the tunnel, faint but echoing, comes the sound of approaching footsteps.

I crawl back to Keith. 'She's coming,' I whisper.

We both look round for somewhere to hide. But already, even from where we are, we can hear the approaching footsteps . . . already they're at the gap in the wire . . . And already I've bent down and pressed my face into the ground so that I can't see the fate that's going to overtake me. Like Milly playing hide-and-seek. Like a little baby.

Then slowly the approaching footsteps fade away again. Slowly I realise that the world hasn't ended, after all.

'Quick!' whispers Keith. 'She's gone past! She's going up the Lanes!'

I sit up. He's already scrambling towards the wire. I scramble hurriedly after him. More ashamed of myself than ever. But I can't help seeing, as he turns to squeeze through the gap, that there's a green grass stain down his cheek. He was hiding his face, just like me. Two little babies together. For a fleeting instant I feel triumphant vindication. Then I'm running home – and realising, halfway back to the tunnel, that Keith's turned the other way, towards the Lanes.

We both stop in surprise. He's going to follow her. Of course. I should have known.

He waits for me to turn back and join him, but I stand my ground. 'What?' he says, smiling his little smile. 'You're frightened of the dogs?'

I shake my head, but still I won't move. I *can't*! She put me on my honour! And I can't explain.

So there we stand – because *he* won't move, either. He won't go without me. And with a flash of pathetic gratitude I realise that he needs me to accompany him. Without me there's no game. Without me there's no one for him to be braver than.

Slowly I walk back to join him.

'Buck up, then,' he says coldly, 'or we'll lose her.'

He begins to trot to catch her up. I trot with him, half a pace behind. Cautiously we slow at every twist and turn of the rutted track, at every opening in the rank green hedgerows where she might be lurking.

Then somewhere ahead of us the dogs begin to bark. Already she's passing the Cottages. We hurry forward.

All summer afternoons in the Lanes seem to labour under a kind of hot dullness and heaviness. Even the train I can hear on the embankment behind us hauls itself over the tunnel and up the gradient towards the cutting with a kind of weariness, as if it's overcome by the same choking green torpor. On the few occasions we've explored along here before, I've always felt we were in another, more ancient and frightening land. As the lane twists left and right, I recognise the sycamore with a rotting length of rope hanging from one of its boughs . . . the sudden little field now choked with sorrel and dock . . . the long patch of nettles . . . a single mouldered and gaping boot . . . an overturned armchair lying in a pool of sodden stuffing . . . Then the Cottages are upon us. And the dogs.

There are three of them, with laid-back, torn ears and evil eyes as varicoloured as their coats, performing the familiar dance of alternating hatred and fear, leaping at us – cowering away – leaping again. At once any remaining differences with Keith are ended, and I'm at his side, or rather just behind his back, trying to conceal myself and the smell of my fear as he turns to face the dogs down, and moves slowly but firmly forwards, with me moving slowly and nervously in step with him.

Our progress is watched expressionlessly by half a dozen children of various ages who are standing in front of the Cottages, in the lane itself or in the little front gardens full of rusting mangles and old mattresses. Their faces are dirty and they're wearing dirty collarless shirts and dirty dresses five sizes too big. Everything about them is plainly laden with germs. They're doing nothing – not playing, not calling off the dogs, not even enjoying our discomfiture – just standing absolutely still, as if they'd been standing there since the beginning of time, and watching us with wooden faces, as if we were members of some quite alien and incomprehensible race – Iron Age invaders in Stone Age territory, white settlers among aborigines.

The uneasy thought comes to me, even in the midst of my fear, that these unreadable and unapproachable creatures hold the key to the mystery. They follow the comings and goings in the Lanes just as we follow the comings and goings in the Close. They've seen X on his way to the hiding place in the tunnel and back. They know what he looks like. They know where he's hiding. But there's no way in which we could ask them, because there's no way in which we can communicate with them.

Keith treats both dogs and children with equal disdain. He examines the Cottages with a slight, pitying smile as we pass, as if they were uninhabited. I pretend to examine them as well, struggling to appear equally condescending. I take in at any rate how low they are, and how grey and blistered their white clapboarding. I note the torn curtains at the windows, and the two small front doors. At either end of the Cottages is a densely cultivated vegetable patch, and at the bottom of each vegetable patch a little tumbledown shed: the privet.

The leaden gaze of the sullen-eyed children weighs on me almost as oppressively as the attentions of the dogs. That same gaze, I realise, has rested a few moments earlier on Keith's mother. An unthinkable thought, which has been lurking for some time now at the back of my mind, slowly takes a slightly more definite shape: that she's here, in the Cottages. That this is the secret knowledge these sly faces are concealing.

One of the front doors opens and a man in a grimy vest emerges. He watches us from the doorstep, chewing something with his mouth open.

X.

Is it?

We keep moving forward, fending off the dogs. It isn't X because it can't be. It can't because . . . because if it is, there's no way in which we can proceed with the matter. Germans we might be able to deal with. These people we certainly can't. We have to believe she's gone further. We have to work on that assumption.

We move slowly on, gazed at and barked at until we're out of sight around the bend. I know that Keith has thought the same unthinkable thought as me, but neither of us makes any reference to it.

We resume our search of every possible entrance into the green confusion on either side. We pass a half-dried-up pond where we once came for tadpoles, then a small, disused chalk pit and a place where the weeds are reclaiming a muddle of collapsed farm carts and broken harrows. The lane peters out into nothingness. A great gap in the earth's furnishings opens in front of us – acre after acre of land stripped bare of its trees and crops, marked out as building lots, then abandoned at the outbreak of war. Now a low savannah of rank weeds has reclaimed the land. The grid of avenues and cul-de-sacs, of roundabouts and turning circles, has disappeared, like the wheel nuts from Keith's father's car and so much else, for the Duration.

'Which way now?' I ask humbly, my voice still not much more than a whisper.

Keith scans the wide horizon of this desolate sea. The only signs of life are tiny figures working on one or two distant islands formed by patches of allotments. Miles away on the other side, like the low cliffs on a far shore, are the last houses in the uncompleted streets where building stopped. What we have to believe is that, from somewhere over there, someone has been coming all the way across this moonscape every evening to check the contents of the croquet box, and that to the same remote destination Keith's mother has now already made the same desolate journey in reverse.

But where, on all that wide shore, is their landfall?

'There must be a path somewhere,' murmurs Keith.

We cast about in the dust where the lane expires. Everywhere among the coarse clumps of vegetation the cracked soil shows through, like the bald pate among the tufts of hair on my father's head, so that there are paths everywhere and nowhere.

We're at the end of the world here, and the same unthinkable thought has returned to both of us. We have to go back to the last place we're sure she reached: the Cottages.

We dawdle about, though, in the vague, nothingy terrain at the end of the Lanes. Still neither of us says anything about the Cottages, and I know Keith's as reluctant as I am, because there's nothing that even he will be brave enough to do when we get there.

Everyone calls the place where we are the Barns, though there are no barns to be seen, only a desolation of overgrown brick footings and collapsed sheets of black corrugated iron, left over from farm buildings that must have fallen down years ago. Even these last traces are beginning to disappear beneath clumps of elder and a wreckage of old enamel bowls with their bottoms hanging out. There was an old tramp living in here somewhere last winter, but Norman Stott says the police took him away. We poke around among the old pots and pans, putting off our return to the Cottages. Keith picks up a flint and throws it at a blackened kettle lying near the low, tumbled brickwork among the elders. It rings out sharply in the silence. I pick up a flint in imitation and throw it, but the kettle remains silent. We've found something to do to keep ourselves occupied for a while. Keith throws another flint, and hits. I throw again and miss.

There's a movement among the elders.

Keith, about to throw for a third hit, lowers his arm. 'The old tramp's back,' he whispers.

We wait. There's no further movement. Keith throws his flint at the elders. It hits some other metal object – something larger and less hollow, by the sound of it. One of the sheets of old corrugated iron that are lying around, perhaps.

Keith creeps closer. I creep with him.

Among the few remaining courses of broken brickwork there seem to be some steps leading down into the ground, either to a secret passageway or to the remains of a cellar. Someone has laid a few sheets of corrugated iron on top of the brick footings so that they make a kind of roof.

'He's down there,' whispers Keith. 'I can hear him.'

I listen, but all I can hear is the sudden, familiar rattle of a train somewhere behind the trees, where the line finally emerges from the long cutting it goes into behind the McAfees. There's something about the offhand, everyday indifference of the sound that makes these dreary woods seem even drearier. I catch the sad, sour smell of the elders in my nostrils, as acrid as cat's pee, and instantly evocative of the soft, pulpy uselessness of the elder's wood, which won't burn on a bonfire, and which feebly snaps if you try to make anything out of it. The hopelessness of the elder's pretensions to be a proper tree – its humiliating position at the very bottom of the hierarchy of trees – seems curiously appropriate to the way the familiar world finally gutters out here at the end of the Lanes. We've come on a journey from the highest to the lowest – from the silver-framed heroes on the altars in the Haywards' house; through the descending social gradation of the Close, from the Berrills and Geests to us; from us to the Pinchers; on down through the squalors of the Cottages and their wretched occupants; and then reached even lower, to an old derelict taking refuge under a sheet of corrugated iron in a stinking elder bush, without even a dog to speak up for him. Without even a privet to go to the lavatory in.

Where does he do it? On the ground somewhere, like an animal. I can smell it, mixing with the smell of the elder. I can feel the germs coming off it.

The sound of the train has died away. And now I do hear something. Coughing. Very quiet coughing. He's trying not to let us hear him. He's scared. Scared of Keith, scared of *me*. He's *that* low in the table of human precedence.

At once, after all my cowardice in the Lanes, I'm brave. I look around for an instrument I can use to make the old man a little more frightened still. 'What?' whispers Keith. I say nothing. I go across to one of the heaps of old pots and pans, and drag out a bent and rusty iron bar. I'm taking the lead for once. I'm showing Keith that he's not the only one who can think of plans and projects.

I reach out with the bar and tap gently on the corrugated iron above the old man's head. The quiet coughing ceases at once. He's prepared to suffocate rather than let us know he's there.

I tap again. Silence.

Keith looks round and finds an old, grey piece of wood that seems to have split away from a fence post. He taps on the corrugated iron with it in his turn.

Silence.

I tap. He taps. Still no response. Still the old tramp's holding his breath down there.

I bring the bar down on the corrugated iron as hard as I can. Keith does the same with his piece of wood. We rain blows down, until the iron begins to dent. The sound fills our heads so that we don't have to think about the inconclusive end of our expedition, and the prospect of going back to the Cottages. It fills the great desolation at the end of the Lanes with human purpose and activity.

If it's as loud as this out here, what must it be like *underneath* the corrugated iron? I can't help laughing at the thought. I can't wait to see the comical terror on the old man's face as he finally comes rushing out and we run off into the Lanes.

He doesn't emerge, though, and in the end we have to stop, panting and laughing too much to continue.

No sign of him. No sound, either, apart from our own commotion, and another train rattling indifferently by behind the trees. It's swallowed up in the depths of the cutting, and the great silence returns.

I remember the time when Dave Avery and some of the boys from round the corner shut poor Eddie Stott up in the dark in the

Hardiments' garden shed, and then beat on the roof. I remember the unearthly animal sounds of Eddie's terror.

The silence from under the corrugated iron is even more unearthly. Not a cry, not a curse, not a breath.

Our laughing has ceased. I feel a sudden chill finger of anxiety touch my heart, and I know that the same sensation is afflicting Keith.

The old man's *not* dead, though. How could he be dead? People don't die from a bit of teasing!

They die from fear, though . . .

Keith throws down his piece of wood. I throw down my iron bar. We don't know quite what to do.

Why don't we go down the steps and look? – Because we can't.

And suddenly we both turn and run, neither of us leader for once, neither of us led.

We run and run, until first the dogs rushing at us and then the children staring at us force us to slow down. Even when we're past the Cottages, and the last of the barking has died away behind us, we say nothing to each other. We walk on past the mouldering boot, past the nettles and the little field of dock and sorrel, past the sycamore with the rope hanging from it, until at last we are out of that skulking, ancient land beyond the tunnel.

We walk silently up the Close. We're silent now because our panic has subsided, and we're both thinking about the old tramp. About the unseen, unheard presence who'd die rather than show his face or let his voice be heard. The unknown who remains unknown. The value in the equation that's yet to be determined. X.

Keith's father is standing at his gate in his Home Guard uniform as we approach.

'Mummy's still not back from Auntie Dee's,' he snaps at Keith. 'I've got a parade this evening. Early supper. She hasn't forgotten?'

So his mother's not back. It takes a moment for the implications of this to sink in. Then my stomach turns over. I glance at Keith.

The same thought has occurred to him; his face has gone white. He catches my eye for a moment and looks away. His gaze becomes filmy and vacant. His grey lips twist into one of his father's mirthless smiles.

'Run down the road and remind her, will you?' says Keith's father.

I can't look at Keith. I can't let myself think about what he's going to do, or what he's going to say.

'Don't bother,' says his father. 'Here she is.'

We watch her come up the Close from the corner with her shopping basket. She's hurrying for once, almost running.

'So sorry, Ted,' she says at last, out of breath. 'Your parade – I know. I went to Paradise. Tried everywhere for a rabbit for the weekend. No luck. Ran all the way back.'

Keith turns away in silence and walks towards the house.

'Supper on the table in ten minutes, then, old girl,' says his father. 'All right?'

He follows Keith into the house. The famous bayonet bounces in its scabbard on his khaki buttock.

Keith's mother looks at me as she turns to close the gate behind her. For a moment she stands absolutely still, considering me as she gets her breath back. 'Was it you two?' she says softly.

I look away.

'Oh, Stephen,' she says sadly. 'Oh, Stephen!'

7

So how much did Stephen understand at this point about what was going on?

I'm outside Meadowhurst, the dull new house that was once an overgrown no man's land called Braemar, and I'm gazing fixedly at the second tub of geraniums from the left on the hard standing. It must be occupying almost exactly the same piece of space that Stephen occupied as he sat in the lookout for hours at a time in the days that followed the expedition to the Lanes. Keith had stopped coming out to play, and Stephen was too uneasy about what was going on inside the Haywards' house to knock on his door. So there he sat, on his own. His bottom was resting on the hard dust now hidden beneath the paving stones. His head must have been more or less exactly where those scarlet blossoms are now.

I gaze at them, baffled.

From the living-room window a boy's watching me, as absorbed and intent as I am. He's about the same age as Stephen was then, and he's trying to work out what's going on inside the head of this old man who stands gazing with such insane concentration at a tub of his mother's geraniums. He's thinking that he's never seen me in the Close before. He's remembering all the stories of the thieves who stole the ornamental bird bath from the next-door neighbour's garden, of the sick ghosts who haunt the edges of the familiar world with outstretched hands, of the pedlars he's been warned against who offer all the terrible pleasures that must be refused, of the torturers of children, of the wandering random murderers . . .

I ignore him. I go on thinking about that head over there, the one growing out of the geranium pot. The thing that's so difficult to grasp is that it's the very same head as the one that's here on my shoulders thinking about it – and yet I've still no more idea of what's going on inside it than the boy behind the curtains has about what's going on inside my present head. I imagine that it's a shifting and comfortless tangle of recollection and apprehension. That it keeps recalling the thunderstorm of blows on the black iron and the silence that followed; the look in Keith's mother's eyes as she turned back to him at the gate and asked him her soft question; the x's and exclamation marks; the kisses in the blackout. That it hasn't forgotten the coming dark of the moon.

Impressions . . . fears . . . But what did Stephen *make* of them all? What did he actually *understand*?

What do *I* understand? Now? About anything? Even the simplest things in front of my eyes? What do I understand about the geraniums in that tub?

Only that they're geraniums in a tub. About the biological, chemical, and molecular processes that lie behind that flaunting scarlet, or even the commercial and economic arrangements that create the market in bedding plants, or the sociological, psychological and aesthetic explanations for the planting out of geraniums in general and these geraniums in particular, I understand more or less nothing.

I don't need to. I simply glance in that direction and at once I've got the general story: geraniums in a tub.

I'm not sure, now the question's been raised, if I really understand even what it means to *understand* something.

If Stephen understood anything at all about what was going on, then I think it was this:

That he had betrayed Keith's mother's trust and let her down; that he had made things worse in some kind of way; that everything in the world was more complicated than he had supposed; that she was now caught in the same difficulty as he was about knowing what to think and what to do, the same deep unease.

I ask myself one very simple, basic question as I stare at the geraniums: did Stephen still think that she was a German spy?

My eyes unfocus as I try to recollect; the geraniums become a vague scarlet blur.

So far as I can piece it together, as the heir to Stephen's thoughts, he neither thought she was nor didn't think she was. Without Keith there to tell him what to think, he'd stopped thinking about it at all. Most of the time you don't go around thinking that things are so or not so, any more than you go around understanding or not understanding them. You take them for granted. I've no doubts at all that those geraniums are geraniums, but all the same I'm not actually thinking the thought, 'Those flowers are geraniums,' or 'Those flowers aren't nasturtiums.' I've got other things to occupy my mind, believe me.

Let me come at it another way. Let me ask myself an even simpler question: what did Stephen think she was actually *doing*?

I'm not sure he thought about even this in any very concrete way. What did he think Mr McAfee did, when he went off at the weekend in his special constable's uniform? If the question ever crossed Stephen's mind, he simply assumed that Mr McAfee continued to do what he was doing as he cycled down the road, which was being a special constable. What did Stephen think Mr Gort did? Well, he was a murderer, so presumably he murdered people. I can't recall Stephen ever puzzling over who he murdered and why. What did Stephen's father do? He vanished in the morning, he reappeared in the evening. Vanishing and reappearing seemed a full enough job description for all practical purposes.

What *do* spies do, for all anyone knows or cares? They behave suspiciously. Keith's mother was behaving suspiciously. Wasn't that enough?

In any case, the mystery at the heart of that shifting cloud of simultaneous possibilities was now x, the silent, unseen presence in the Barns. What did Stephen think about him?

He thought that he was a German. The less clear the Germanness of Keith's mother became, the more clearly it was transferred to her courier or controller. The Germanness, revealed by Keith's initial perception, was the source from which the whole sequence of events had taken its rise. It remained, like some residual belief in God amidst a sea of doubt about the theological details, the one sure item of faith that Stephen had to hold on to.

But Stephen also thought that he was an old tramp, since he lived in a place where old tramps lived.

So Stephen thought that he was an old German tramp?

Not at all. The idea that there might be old tramps of German nationality never entered his head. What he thought, as I understand it, was two quite unrelated things with unrelated parts of his mind: that the unseen figure in the Barns was German, and that at the same time he was something quite different – an old tramp.

Though I suspect that in a third part of Stephen's mind there was an unconscious link between being an old tramp and being German that made the two beliefs a little more compatible: the *germs* with which old tramps were presumably covered, and which were presumably so called because they were as evil and insidious as Germans.

Did Stephen think that this ambiguous figure was also Auntie Dee's mysterious boyfriend, as Barbara Berrill had suggested, or that Keith's mother might be kissing him under the black corrugated iron? No – notions of that sort had become more ridiculous than ever. Even if people's aunts had boyfriends, they certainly didn't have boyfriends who were old tramps. Even if people kissed people in the blackout, they certainly didn't kiss germ-laden Germans.

And yet, somewhere in Stephen's mind, the echo of that word 'boyfriend', the ghost of those stolen kisses, lingered like a faint scent in the air.

What he wanted, I think, was for all the shifting thoughts inside his head to cease, for everything to stop happening and to go back to what it had been before. The clean simplicity of espionage, that had promised so well, had turned into such a sticky mess. What he wanted was for Keith to arrive with some new notion, some fresh project that would drive the old one out of both their heads.

He didn't come, though. Stephen was left to sit and think on his own.

Another cause for unease: what had happened to him?

Every time Stephen made up his mind to go and knock on Keith's door as usual, he saw it being opened not by him but his mother, and at the thought of her unspoken reproach, her sad 'Oh, Stephen', he stayed where he was, waiting for Keith to come to him.

I refocus my eyes, and lift them from the geraniums to the boy watching me. What's *he* made of all *his* unease? He's vanished, though – gone to tell his mother about me, no doubt. In a moment she'll come and take a look for herself, and at the sight of me now gazing into her living-room window she'll be phoning the police, as Mrs Hardiment did before when she saw that mysterious intruder lurking about the Close.

I move on. Up the road and across to Keith's house again.

As of course Stephen did then, in the end. There was nothing else for it.

By then, in any case, everything had begun to recede into the past a little, as everything always does. Nothing more had happened. Everything really had perhaps gone back to what it had been before.

It's his mother who opens the door, exactly as I'd feared. I can't lift my eyes to look at her, because all my courage has been exhausted by the effort of walking up the path and knocking on the door, but I have the impression that she's smiling down at me with her old tranquillity. 'Oh, hello, Stephen,' she says, and this time I can detect no shadow of reproach. 'We haven't seen you round here for some time.'

I utter the recognised formula, my eyes still on the ground. 'Can Keith come out to play?'

For a moment she hesitates. Then she turns to call towards the upstairs landing. 'Keith, darling! It's Stephen!' She turns back to me and I feel another smile bent upon me. 'Why don't you go up, Stephen? He's just tidying the playroom.'

I step into the hall, and the quiet, familiar order recomposes itself around me once again: the hall stand with the clothes brushes and shoe horns . . . the rack with the sticks and canes . . . the Trossachs . . . the pagodas . . . From somewhere outside the house the endless solo for pursed human lips comes and goes as Keith's father passes and repasses about his business in the garden. Keith's mother watches me as I climb the familiar stairs, and the grandmother clock chimes the quarter.

Yes, everything's back to what it was.

Keith's sitting on the floor of the playroom sorting the elements of a construction kit into the appropriate compartments of its box. He looks up briefly as I come in. 'Watch where you put your feet, old chap,' he says.

I sit down on the floor opposite him. He goes on with his work, saying nothing, as if there were nothing surprising about my having been absent, or having now returned. I think this is what he means – that nothing unusual has happened after all. He's telling me the game's over. The question of his mother's espionage, which once seemed so urgent, has turned out to be too difficult to resolve. It's been put into the archives and forgotten, like so many other questions that seemed so urgent in their time. Neither of us will ever refer to it again. He has found the solution to all that stickiness and unease, just as I knew he would.

I breathe in the sweet, familiar perfumes of the room: the metallic briskness of the flanges and brackets in the construction kit and the shiny, cardboard cleanness of the box it came in; the sharp, nose-tickling intoxications of the spirit glue that holds the wings on the model aircraft, of the acetone solvent of their camouflage; the quiet seriousness of the light machine oil that lubricates so many well-maintained bearings in so many models and motors.

'Shall we go on building the railway?' I suggest. 'Shall we do the viaduct over that gorge in the mountains?'

I'm telling him that I understand. I'm agreeing that we never strained our ears in terrible silence at the Barns, that the marks in the diary meant nothing, and that the dark of the moon will come and go without event. I'm promising him that I shan't refer to these things any more than he will, that I gladly accept his solution, that I too know the game's over.

He goes on putting struts with struts and flanges with flanges. The perfect tidiness of the room becomes gradually more perfect still. 'I've got to pipeclay my cricket stuff when I've finished this,' he says.

I watch him. He's ignoring my dull suggestion about the viaduct, of course, since it came from me and not from him. He's suddenly going to get a completely new idea into his head out of nowhere. He's going to lead us into some new project, and I can't wait to find out what it will be.

There's a tap on the door, and his mother looks into the room. 'I'm just popping round to Auntie Dee's,' she says. 'You chaps will be all right on your own, will you?'

Everything's back to normal; she's popping round to Auntie Dee's just as she's always done.

After she's gone Keith still says nothing. He keeps his eyes on the work in hand. He's concentrating, like me, on the normality of his mother's routine. He's concentrating on seeing her walk up the path to Auntie Dee's, and not round the corner at the end of the road, or through the tunnel, or into the Lanes.

Everything's back to normal; but we both privately know that what's normal has changed, and changed for ever. The game's over because the normal has reached out to absorb the abnormal. The story has changed tack, like a ship altering course, and now it sails on as straight and level as it did before, but to a different destination – and we're no longer aboard.

Keith puts the construction kit away, and gets his cricket pads and boots out of the cupboard. I trail downstairs after him, and watch him spread everything out on sheets of newspaper in the yard. The back door of the garage on the other side of the yard is open, and from it comes another range of familiar smells: sawdust, motor oil, swept concrete, car. His father's huge shadow, cast by the low light over the workbench, moves around the walls inside, like an ogre in his cave, over the tennis rackets and the other neatly suspended mementoes of their pre-war life, whistling, whistling.

I watch the grey smudges and green grass stains on the pad disappear beneath the first stripe of perfect whiteness. It comes to me that there's going to be no new idea, no new game. The new normality doesn't include them. It's not just the one game that's over; all our games are over. I'm the accomplice in a crime which is as indeterminate as those smudges and stains, but which is now being painted out, and I along with them.

'I'd probably better go home,' I say miserably. 'It must be nearly supper time.'

'All right.' Another moistly gleaming stripe of whiteness appears. Still I linger.

'Are you coming out to play tomorrow?' I ask.

'I don't know. I'll have to see.'

He suddenly straightens up. The whistling in the garage has ceased. I turn round, and see his father watching us from the doorway of the garage, his lips drawn back in the familiar thin, impatient smile.

'Thermos,' he says.

He's talking to Keith, of course. He's given no more sign than he ever does of noticing my presence. I look at Keith. He goes red. He's being accused of a crime, and already he's feeling guilty – doubly guilty, because he knows he should be able to guess immediately what the crime is, and he can't.

His father waits. Keith goes redder still.

'Come on, old bean,' says his father impatiently, and I feel a lurch of fear for myself as well as Keith. 'Thermos flask. In the picnic hamper. Anyone say you could take it?'

Keith looks at the ground. 'I didn't take it.'

Another little smile from his father. 'Taking other people's things without permission – that's stealing. You know that. Saying you didn't when you did – that's lying. Yes?'

Keith goes on looking at the ground. In the silence the words 'Mummy must have taken it' hang in the air unsaid, audible only to Keith and me.

'Where is it, then, old bean?'

Another silence, three syllables long: 'In the Barns.'

'Don't be a blithering idiot. Some game you're playing? Best be a man and own up.'

The silence is heavy with the same explanation – twice over, unsaid by Keith and unsaid by me.

'I'm disappointed in you,' says his father. The smile's worse now; there's sorrow and pity in it. All at once I realise what he really suspects: that *I've* taken the thermos. That Keith's protecting me.

'You know what you're going to get, old bean,' says his father. 'Wash that stuff off your hands. Dry them properly.'

He goes in through the kitchen door, wiping his shoes on the mat.

'You'd better go,' says Keith to me. He's still red in the face, still not looking at anything except the ground. He follows his father into the kitchen, also wiping his shoes on the mat, and I hear the sound of the water splashing in the sink as he washes the white cleaner off his hands to prepare them.

I'd gladly leave, as Keith told me, but I can't, because I have to go in and confront his father. I have to stop this thing happening. I have to tell him that he's right – that *I* took the thermos.

I did, after all. In effect. I betrayed her trust. I made her go to the Barns. Something bad's happening there, and I'm the one who made it happen. The game's not over. It's simply become a more terrible kind of game.

Silence from the house. I must go and tell him.

The silence goes on and on. I must.

Keith's father comes out of the kitchen and goes back into the garage. He begins to whistle again.

Keith reappears. The redness in his cheeks has turned blotchy. His hands are pressed beneath his armpits.

'I told you to go, old bean,' he says shortly.

'I'm sorry,' I whisper abjectly. I'm sorry for not going, for not owning up, for seeing him like this, for going now and leaving him like this, for the stinging in his hands; for everything.

His father comes out of the garage again. 'I'll give you until bedtime to think about it,' he says to Keith. 'If it's not back by then you'll get the same again. And then again tomorrow. And so on every day until it's back.'

He lingers in the doorway, looking at the ground, thinking about something else.

'And your mother's at Auntie Dee's again?' he asks finally, in a different tone. Keith nods.

The little smile comes back to his father's lips. He goes back into the garage. The grindstone whirrs and there's a sudden shower of sparks. I can't see what he's sharpening, but I don't need to because I know. It's the bayonet, the famous bayonet.

I start running towards the end of the road. I don't think I have any clear idea of what I'm going to do – I just know that I have to do *something*. Something to make amends at last for all my betrayals and failures. Something bold and decisive that will save Keith from his father, and avert the catastrophe I can feel looming, though what that catastrophe might be I don't know.

At the very least I have to get the thermos flask back in the picnic hamper before bedtime comes and Keith's caned again. I turn the corner towards the tunnel. I suppose I'm running in the direction of the Barns. I don't think I'm intending to go all the way there. So far as I can tell I'm intending to be lucky enough to meet her on the way.

My plan carries itself out even before I've had a chance to find out more precisely what it is. As I run out of the sunshine into the roaring darkness of the tunnel I collide full tilt with someone running out of it. We seize hold of each other, my face buried in a soft confusion of bosoms, and dance a precarious tango together to keep our footing on the muddy shore of the great subterranean lake. We chassé one way into the wetness of the wall, then the other way into the wetness of the water. When we recover ourselves, and struggle back off the darkened dance floor into the sunlight outside, all her tranquil dignity has evaporated.

'Stephen!' she cries, bending to scramble together the tumbled clothes and books that have fallen out of her basket into the mud.

'The thermos,' I say.

'What did I tell you, Stephen?' she says, as angry as she was the night she first got the slime of the tunnel on her clothes. 'What did I ask you? Why are you doing this?'

'The thermos,' I repeat desperately.

'You're a very naughty boy, Stephen, and I'm very cross with you.'

'The thermos flask!'

At last she takes in what I'm saying. She looks at me intently.

'What do you mean?' she asks in a different voice. 'What's happened?'

And now my tongue's tied by a ticklish point of social semantics. I can't get started on telling her what's happened because I don't know how to refer to the person concerned. Do I say, 'Keith's father'? I can't talk about Keith's father to Keith's mother! He must have some more direct relationship to her. The word 'husband' comes to mind. Can I say 'your husband'? No, it's even more unsayable. 'Mr Hayward'? Worse still.

She's already guessed, though. 'Ted said something about it?' she asks quietly. All I have to do is nod – and already she's guessed the rest of the story as well.

'He doesn't think Keith took it?' I nod.

She bites her lip. Her brown eyes are fixed on me.

'He didn't punish him?' I nod.

'Caned him?' I nod yet again.

She winces, as if it was her own hands that were red hot.

'Oh, Stephen,' she says, as she said before. 'Oh, Stephen!'

From never saying my name at all, she's gone to saying it more often than everybody else in the world put together.

'And he's told Keith to put it back?' she asks softly.

'By bedtime,' I manage.

She looks at her watch, then begins to walk back into the tunnel. Her pale summer dress is streaked with green slime, and her white summer sandals squelch muddily at every step. I've tried to preserve her secret, and I've written it all over her.

She stops and turns.

'Thank you, Stephen,' she says humbly.

8

What's going to happen now?

I walk to the lookout each evening after school, breathing in all the disturbing new sweetnesses that fill the air of the Close as the midsummer draws on: the light and easy innocence of the pleached limes in front of the Hardiments and the honeysuckle in front of Mr Gort's house and the Geests; the sleepy, treacly richness of the buddleia hanging out over the pavement of the Stotts and the McAfees; the refined delicacy of feeling of the Haywards' standard roses. Then I sit on my own, gazing helplessly at the outside of Keith's house.

The only thing I know for sure is that I now really am shut out of that well-ordered world for ever. Never again will I hear the chiming of the clocks, or eat chocolate spread in the gleam of the polished silverware. The family has closed in upon itself. Once or twice I see a curtain twitch as it's drawn against the afternoon sun, or Mrs Elmsley wheeling her bicycle out from the back yard and setting off home. Sometimes Keith comes past on his way home from school and wheels his bicycle in. Once Keith's father comes round the side of the house with a hose, whistling, whistling, and waters the front garden. Of his mother there's no sign.

Something's going on in there, I know that. With half my mind I expect to see a policeman cycle up to the house, as he did to Auntie Dee's. With the other half I expect nothing to happen at all.

Nothing does. So is she simply lying low, waiting to resume her activities when we get to the dark of the moon? I feel as if I've been left to decide the fate of the world singlehanded. I realise I should tell someone about it. A grown-up. Let them sort it out. Tell them what, though? – What's going on. – But I don't know what *is* going on!

Tell which grown-up, anyway? Mr McAfee, as we did with Mr Gort? I imagine Mr McAfee looking at the schoolboy handwriting as he did before, even with his name spelt right this time, and at once I lose heart.

My family? I lurk about in the kitchen when my mother's making supper, standing close to her as she works, wondering whether the words will come out.

'What *is* it?' she demands impatiently. 'You're always under my feet! What do you want?'

I retire to the bedroom, where my brother's sitting with his homework open in front of him, trying to get the nicotine stains off his fingers with a pumice stone before our mother notices them.

'I wish you wouldn't keep wandering in and out,' he says. 'I'm trying to work. It's hell's own distracting.'

Or my father. I don't even have to wait for him to come home to know what he'd say: 'Shnick-shnack!'

And when I try to imagine the words coming out of my mouth I can hear the horrible sneaking tone they'd have. It would be telling tales. We told on Mr Gort, of course. But then that wasn't true in the same way as this is true. Or might be true. So telling tales is worse than spying? Worse than letting someone put the lives of our soldiers and sailors at risk?

And of our airmen. I see Uncle Peter standing at the gate holding Milly and laughing, with all the rest of us crowding round to feel the hard embroidery of the leaves beneath the eagle, and the softness of the red velvet cushions in the crown, and I think, no, we shall never touch that embroidery again, or those spots of red – because I've allowed him to be shot down . . .

I tear a page out of one of my exercise books. 'Dear Mr McAfee,' I write, and stop. Perhaps it will be all right if I don't make any direct accusation or insinuation – if I simply describe what I've seen and leave him to decide what to make of it. 'I saw Keith Hayward's mother,' I write. 'She put something in a box by the tunnel, and I looked and there was a sock inside . . .' I tear it up. 'The old tramp is back in the Barns, only it's a German, and Keith Hayward's mother was in there with him . . .'

My palms sweat. It's telling tales, there's no getting away from it.

So I sit in the sweet air under the bushes on my own, watching and waiting. I even call out to the Stotts' dog as it passes, and think of ways to keep it hanging around and taking an interest in me. I'm so intent on the dog that Barbara Berrill's inside the lookout before I realise.

'I always know if you're hiding in here,' she says.

I feel too miserable even to tell her to go away. I fiddle with a dead twig while she settles herself next to me, her maddening blue school purse with the blue popper still dangling round her neck.

'You're on your own all the time these days,' she says. 'Aren't you and Keith friends any more?'

I've no intention of replying to this, of course – and anyway at this very instant, with the natural contrariness of events, Keith comes down the garden path from the Haywards' kitchen door and opens the front gate. My heart leaps twice, once for joy and once for fear.

'Don't worry,' whispers Barbara Berrill. 'He's not coming here. He's going shopping.'

This is plainly nonsense. Keith has never gone shopping in his life. But as he closes the gate behind him and turns, I see the basket on his arm. He walks down the road without so much as a glance at the lookout.

'He's always doing the shopping for his Mummy these days,' whispers Barbara Berrill. 'And for Mrs Tracey.'

Keith goes into Auntie Dee's front gate and knocks at her door. I feel a ridiculous little sour spurt of jealousy. How does Barbara Berrill know about Keith's new habits when I don't?

Auntie Dee opens the door and smiles. She's holding a piece of paper to show him. She was evidently expecting him.

'I think something funny must have happened,' says Barbara Berrill. 'Mrs Hayward always used to be running round to Mrs

Tracey's. She never goes there now. Why not? Have they fallen out or something?'

I've no idea. Whatever's happened, though, I know it's my fault. My jealousy's overtaken by guilt.

'Or don't you know what goes on at the Haywards any more?' says Barbara Berrill. 'You never go there now, do you?'

She's just twisting the knife, and I refuse to let myself feel it. I keep my eyes fixed on Auntie Dee, who's going through a list on her piece of paper with Keith, pencil in hand, amending items and adding fresh ones.

Barbara Berrill puts her hand over her mouth and giggles. 'Perhaps Mrs Hayward's got a boyfriend, too, like Mrs Tracey,' she says. I can feel her looking at me to see if she's made my face go funny again, but nothing she says can shock me any more. 'And Keith's Daddy's found out, and now he won't let her set foot outside the house.'

I keep my eyes on Keith. He takes the list, and sets out for the end of the road. Barbara Berrill puts her mouth very close to my ear. 'And perhaps,' she whispers, 'she makes Keith take messages to him for her. Perhaps that's where he's going now!'

I know perfectly well that this is just a further example of the stupid things that girls say, but even so another, still sourer tide of jealousy sweeps through my veins. Exactly where this jealousy's directed I couldn't say. Is it of Barbara Berrill for claiming the right to make knowing speculations about the behaviour of my friend? Or of Keith for supplanting me in his mother's confidence? Or even of his mother herself, for having this supposed boyfriend of hers?

Another whisper in my ear: 'Shall we follow him and see who it is?'

Now she's trying to supplant Keith as the one who makes the plans and projects! And the plans and projects are actually directed against Keith! I turn at last to express my indignation, but before I can speak she's laid a hand on my arm and pointed silently at Keith's house. The front door has opened, and Keith's mother's coming out. She has some letters in her hand; she's still allowed to go to the post, at any rate. We both watch intently, everything else forgotten, as she pulls the door very gently to behind her.

'She's *creeping* out,' whispers Barbara Berrill.

Keith's mother walks down the garden path to the front gate, not creeping now, but as tranquil and unhurried as ever . . . but then stops, and turns back towards the house. Keith's father has appeared from the back yard, wearing his engineer's overalls and holding a paintbrush.

'Oh no!' whispers Barbara Berrill.

He walks slowly towards Keith's mother, and they talk for some moments.

'They're having a terrible quarrel,' whispers Barbara Berrill.

So far as I can see they're talking quietly and reasonably, a couple like any other couple in the street settling some small point of domestic routine.

Keith's father goes back into the yard. Keith's mother remains standing by the garden gate, the letters in her hand, gazing calmly up into the serene blue depths of the evening sky above her head.

'She doesn't know what to do,' whispers Barbara Berrill. 'She doesn't know whether to go or not.'

Keith's mother stands for a long time, searching the sky for an answer to her problems.

'Is it because of her boyfriend that you and Keith aren't friends any more?' asks Barbara Berrill.

Keith's father reappears. He's taken off his overalls and put on a shirt and flannels. He opens the garden gate, ushers Keith's mother through, and they stroll down the street together.

Barbara Berrill giggles. 'Oh no! He's even going to the letter box with her!'

Yes. This is what they were discussing – this is why he's changed his clothes. The summer evening's so fine that he's been tempted into an affectionate gesture of a quite unheard-of nature. He's torn himself away from the workbench and the garden for once to accompany her on her stroll to the post.

Barbara Berrill's right. When Keith's mother finally reached home that day with her white dress badged with green slime, the situation changed. There's no slime on the way to the shops, or the post, or Auntie Dee's house. Whatever story she told Keith's father to explain it, that slime must have suddenly seemed to touch all her absences. So now he has turned the key on her. She has become a prisoner. All possibility of contact with the world beyond the tunnel has been destroyed.

They saunter down the street, and stop to breathe the scent of the honeysuckle in front of Mr Gort's house. She casts a brief glance in our direction, as if wondering what any possible observer might make of all this, and all I can think is that we seem to have defeated her. Without any drama or scandal, we have brought her career as a spy to an end.

Or *I* have.

They saunter on, but at once she stops again. She steadies herself against Keith's father's arm and lifts one impeccable white sandal from the ground to examine the heel strap. There seems to be something wrong with it. They talk, as quietly and offhandedly as before, then she hands him the letters and walks back towards the house, stopping again on the way to ease the strap.

'She's just pretending,' breathes Barbara Berrill in my ear.

He watches her until she's gone through the front gate, then looks at the addresses on the envelopes and resumes his stroll to the corner. She stops just inside the gate, her attention apparently caught by something in the sky again.

Somehow she still seems to be holding one of the letters.

'She's just hiding till he's gone. Then she's going to . . .'

Going to what?

She opens the gate, casts one brief look towards the corner, and comes straight across the road towards us.

'Oh, *no*!' squeaks Barbara Berrill, and ducks her head. I automatically imitate her.

'Stephen?' says Keith's mother quietly through the leaves. 'May I come in?'

I have to straighten up and look at her. So does Barbara Berrill. Keith's mother looks from one to the other, disconcerted.

'Oh, hello, Barbara,' she says. 'I'm so sorry. I thought Stephen was on his own.'

She starts back across the street, then hesitates and returns. She smiles.

'I was just going to say, you must come to tea again some time, Stephen.'

She goes back to her house. At any rate her sandal no longer seems to be troubling her.

'She wanted you to take him that letter, didn't she?' whispers Barbara Berrill. '*Would* you have, Stephen? If she'd asked you? If I hadn't been here?'

I put my hands over my head and gaze at the dust. I don't know what I should have done. I don't know anything about anything.

Barbara Berrill laughs. 'We could have found out where he lived. We could have found out who it was.'

Where he lives is the one thing I think I do know. Who it might be is something I'm not sure I want to investigate any more closely.

I suppose there's one other thing I have such a strong foreboding of that it almost counts as knowing: she's going to come back and try asking me again.

'If you and Keith aren't friends any more,' says Barbara Berrill finally, 'can I see inside your secret box thing?'

A little tangle of children hovers around Auntie Dee's gate. I see them as I turn the corner on my way home from school next day, and I walk up the street to investigate with my satchel still on my shoulder.

All the younger children in the Close are there, except of course Keith, who never plays with the others: the Geest twins, Barbara Berrill, Norman and Eddie, Dave Avery – even Elizabeth Hardiment and Roger have abandoned their practice for once. They're all reverently touching a heavy, upright bicycle that stands propped against the gatepost with a policeman's cape looped tidily over the handlebars.

As soon as they see me, everyone starts talking at once.

'That man was hanging round again last night!'

'The peeping Tom!'

'In the blackout!'

'Barbara's Mummy saw him!'

Poor Eddie Stott laughs in delight at all the excitement. Everyone else looks respectfully at Barbara Berrill, honouring her association with her mother's importance. She smiles enigmatically, but says nothing, and gives me a specially significant glance to indicate that she and I share a secret understanding of who the man is and why he came.

'He had a beard!' resume the others.

'He had these awful staring eyes!'

'She couldn't see! It was dark!'

'She *could* see! In the moonlight!'

'And she screamed!'

'And he ran away!'

'He ran into Trewinnick!'

'He preys on women,' announces Elizabeth Hardiment, and her words carry authority because she wears glasses.

'Of course,' explains Roger Hardiment, who also wears glasses. 'Because he's a sexual deviant.'

Eddie laughs and claps his hands.

I glance at Barbara Berrill again. She gives me a solemnly excited look. She's telling me that she's resisting the urge to announce to everyone what she knows, and she's doing it for my sake, because Keith's my friend and she's mine.

'He's coming out!' whispers one of the Geest twins, and we all spin round to look at Auntie Dee's house. It's not the staring-eyed deviant, of course – it's the policeman, being shown out of the front door by Auntie Dee. He turns back to say something to her. She nods silently, biting her lip, her ever-smiling face for once pinched and anxious.

134

'Oh, no!' whispers one of the Geest twins. 'Look at her!'

'She's really frightened,' whispers the other.

'Because if the man's come back once,' explains Elizabeth Hardiment, 'she knows he'll come back again.'

'Sexual deviants always do,' says Roger Hardiment.

As the policeman comes back to the garden gate and Auntie Dee starts to close the door, she notices us all watching her. She opens it wide again and waves, all smiles as usual.

Dave Avery, Norman Stott, and Roger Hardiment rush forward and stand the policeman's bicycle upright for him. Everyone watches him, waiting for him to make some pronouncement on the case. He has a thick, gingery moustache which turns down at the ends and gives him an important look, but he says nothing. We all stand back and silently follow as he wheels the bicycle up the street.

'He's going to Trewinnick,' whispers one of the Geest twins.

'*Are* you?' the other one asks him boldly.

No answer.

'Dad's seen the people who live in there,' Dave Avery informs him.

'They're never there in the day,' explains Norman Stott.

'They only go there at night.'

I peer past the evergreens into the overgrown garden with everyone else as we approach. The blackout curtains at the windows are drawn, and the usual melancholy neglect reigns undisturbed.

'That man's probably still hiding round the back somewhere,' whispers one of the Geests.

Barbara Berrill looks at me to see how I react to the possibility of his imminent discovery. All the unease I felt before reawakens.

The policeman walks straight past Trewinnick, though.

Half a dozen fingers point out his mistake. 'There! No! That one!'

He props his bicycle against the Haywards' gatepost. Of course.

'Keith's house,' whispers everyone, and they all turn to look at me, because Keith's my friend, so I have some kind of responsibility for what goes on here. I say nothing, and try not to catch anyone's eye, but I feel the blood coming to my face.

They all turn back to watch silently as the policeman bangs twice with the heavy knocker.

'It's because Mrs Hayward's Mrs Tracey's sister,' explains Elizabeth Hardiment.

'Yes, or when the man ran into Trewinnick he climbed over the fence, and started to prey on Mrs Hayward instead,' says Roger Hardiment.

They sneak another look at me. I keep my gaze fixed on the house, but then have to look away when Keith's mother opens the front door. I don't want to see what expression she has on her face as the policeman explains why he's come.

Eventually she stands back, and the policeman scrapes his boots on the scraper, then steps inside and wipes them again on the mat, just as I do. The front door closes. I should do something, I know. I should go and knock on the door and tell the policeman everything I know. But all I do is stand there, gazing at the closed front door with everyone else, trying not to imagine what's going on beyond it, trying not to be aware of Barbara Berrill looking sideways at me.

Then we all turn and fall back, because someone's waiting to get past us to the gate. It's Keith, dismounting from his bicycle on his way home from school, smiling his father's little thin smile of embarrassment to find his home besieged. We watch in silence as he manoeuvres awkwardly to open the gate and wheel his bicycle in. I should step forward and help him. I should explain what's going on. I do nothing, though. It's the Geests who are left to take pity on him.

'The policeman's here,' says one of them. 'He's talking to your Mummy.'

'That peeping Tom was hanging around again last night,' says the other.

'He's a sexual deviant,' says Roger Hardiment. 'He's preying on your mother.'

Keith says nothing. For a moment our eyes meet, and I see the eyelids come down in the familiar curtain of contempt. I've ceased to be his friend; I've become one of the mob. I glance away quickly, and catch Barbara Berrill watching both of us.

'Why won't he say anything?' demands Norman Stott, looking at me, as Keith pushes his bicycle up the path and disappears into the back yard.

'Because he's worried about his Mummy,' says one of the Geests.

'No, he's not,' says Dave Avery. 'He's just stuck up.'

They all look at me.

'He won't even speak to *you* now!' says a Geest.

'Perhaps he's the peeping Tom,' says Dave Avery.

'Or perhaps Stephen is,' says Norman Stott slyly. Eddie beams trustingly up into my face and tries to take my hand.

I don't respond to either of them. I concentrate on trying not to imagine Keith putting his bicycle away in the shed . . . taking his books out of the saddlebag . . . coming into the hall where his father's listening without comment while his mother tells the policeman that she hasn't noticed anything unusual. I refuse to see Keith going red in the face and smiling his father's smile as they all three turn to look at him . . .

The front door opens, and Keith's mother sees the policeman out. She's wearing a helpful smile. She's told him that she'll let the police know at once if she sees anything suspicious.

Keith's father has gone back to his workbench, Keith has gone up to his playroom. Nothing has been said. Nothing awkward is going to occur.

The children hand the policeman his bicycle and run beside him as he rides slowly away towards the end of the Close. I wait for them to go, then I crawl into the lookout and sit there with my head in my hands. Once again I've done nothing. Nothing to help her. Nothing to stop her.

'It wasn't Auntie Dee's boyfriend this time, was it?' whispers Barbara Berrill. She's sitting in the observation post watching me, catching at the flap of her purse with her lower lip, making the popper pop and unpop. 'It was Keith's Mummy's boyfriend. Because Keith's Daddy won't let her out of his sight. He came to see her.'

I go on fiddling with the same dead twig that I was fiddling with before, breaking it into small pieces. Life's going round in circles.

'Mummy got in such a state last night!' whispers Barbara Berrill. 'She went out to look for Deirdre, because it was almost dark and Deirdre still hadn't come home, and she was raving about Daddy not being there to keep us in order and look after us – then suddenly she saw this man, and she thought, "Oh, no!"'

I break the pieces of twig into smaller pieces still.

'Actually,' she whispers, 'I know why Deirdre hadn't come home.'

I can feel her looking at me, to see if I know as well. Of course I do, though I'm not going to say.

'She was with your brother somewhere.'

'I know,' I say, before I remember I'm not going to.

'And I know what they were doing,' she whispers.

'They smoke cigarettes,' I say in spite of myself, unable to let her think I don't know something that she does.

No reply. I glance at her. She's still looking at me, smiling secretly. She has some extra piece of knowledge that she's longing to impart.

'They kiss each other,' she whispers. 'Deirdre told me. They smoke cigarettes and then they kiss each other.'

'I know, I know,' I say, though I didn't. But I can perfectly well believe it now I do know. It's just about what Geoff *would* do.

Barbara holds the blue purse in front of her mouth, still popping and unpopping it, and looking at me over the top of it.

'Your face has gone all squidgy again,' she says.

'No, it hasn't.'

'You can't see.'

She's still looking at me.

'Have *you* ever smoked cigarettes?' she whispers.

'Loads.'

'I bet you haven't.'

'Yes, I have. Loads and loads.'

She smiles at me, not believing me but pretending to because she wants to talk about it. 'Is it nice?'

I try to remember what it was actually like when Charlie Avery and I manufactured two cigarettes out of the sodden tobacco from the ends in his parents' ashtrays. All I can recall is the deliciously forbidden indoor-firework smell of the flaring match. I shrug. 'Quite nice.'

'Do you smoke cigarettes in here with Keith?' she asks. She's holding up something she's found on the ground beside her. It's a cigarette that someone has started to smoke and then stubbed out. I'm too taken aback by the sight to claim the credit for it in time. 'Somebody else must have been in here, then,' she says.

I feel a kind of vertigo. I've lost any grip I ever had on the world. Strangers are coming into our special place, and whispering and pleading and telling secrets and smoking cigarettes, and I've no control over any of it.

Barbara inspects the cigarette. 'It's a cork tip,' she says. She puts it between her lips and pretends to smoke it, giggling.

'You'll get germs!' I cry, shocked. 'You don't know where it's been!'

She takes it out of her mouth and languorously blows an imaginary smoke ring. 'I can guess,' she says. She blows another smoke ring.

It takes me a moment to guess what her guess is. I gaze at her, still more disturbed. What – Geoff and Deirdre? In the dark? Smoking? And kissing each other? In *here*?

'I bet it was,' she says. 'Have you got any matches?'

I don't rise to this, at any rate. She's only asking because she knows I haven't.

She nods at the padlocked trunk. 'What about in your secret box thing?'

I hesitate for an instant as I suddenly remember the candle stub and the matches to light it, then shake my head. My instant of hesitation was too long, though.

'Come on,' she says. 'He won't know.'

She leans across me and tries the padlock. My lap's full of the weight and softness of her, and the movements of her body as she pulls the padlock back and forth. The blue purse has come to rest on top of my hand. I can feel the bobbliness of the leather and the shininess of the popper against my skin, and the wetness on the edge of the flap where she was catching it against her lip.

'Where's the key?' she demands. I say nothing. She turns her head and looks up at me, her head mockingly upside down, her hair falling in her eyes. 'Or doesn't he let you have the key?'

My sense of vertigo returns. There's no firm ground anywhere. I roll sideways under her and get the key out from under the hidden stone. I hear the soft, smooth sounds as she turns it in the lock that Keith keeps so carefully oiled. She lifts the lid and gazes at the contents.

'These are all your secret things?' she says. She picks up various items, still lying in my lap. I watch her helplessly. The enormity of my crime is almost too much to comprehend. First I let a stranger into our private place – and now I let her see our most private possessions. How has this happened?

'Are these pretend bullets?'

'No, they're real ones.'

'Why have you got an old sock in here?'

I take it away from her and throw it back. 'We need it for something special.'

She takes out the carving knife. 'What's this for?'

'It's a bayonet.'

'A *bayonet*?' She cautiously feels the edges. 'You mean for sticking into people?'

Yes, and for administering the oath to reveal nothing of all this to any living soul, and for cutting my throat if I break the oath, so help me God and hope to die. I say nothing more.

'The handle's come off,' she says. 'It looks more like a carving knife to me.'

It looks more like a carving knife to me, too. I take it away from her and put it carefully back in the trunk. She sits up and shows me what she's found in its place – the box of matches. She strikes one, and I feel the thrilling prickle of the firework fumes in my nose. She puts the cigarette back in her mouth, and cautiously advances the bent and blackened end into the flame. Her face glows in the flickering light. Two tiny images of fire dance in the darkness of her narrowed eyes.

Suddenly she drops the match and snatches the cigarette out of her mouth, choking and coughing. 'Ugh!' she cries, looking at it in astonishment. 'It's absolutely beastly!'

I hold out my hand. 'Let me have a go.'

She ignores me. With infinite precaution she puts the cigarette back into her mouth and tries again. Again she chokes and coughs, and gets the smoke in her eyes as well. This time she blindly hands the cigarette to me, and presses her eyes against the backs of her hands.

I put the cigarette into my mouth. The cork tip is moist from her lips, like the flap of her purse. Very carefully I suck in a little smoke. I feel the presence of it inside my mouth, as if it were something solid. She takes her hands away from her eyes and watches me, weeping and blinking. I hold the smoke in my mouth for a few moments, careful not to get it into my throat. It tastes of importance and of being grown up. I lift my head, as I've seen Geoff do, and blow the smoke out again. I sigh with satisfaction.

She takes the cigarette back. 'How do you do it?' she asks humbly.

'You just have to get used to it.'

She screws up her eyes and takes another little puff.

'Now blow it out,' I instruct her. She blows the smoke out, and jerks her head back to keep her eyes away from it.

She hands me the cigarette, and watches as I take another little mouthful.

'Do you feel all right?' she asks. 'It's supposed to make you feel sick.'

Do I feel all right? I feel . . . *something* disturbing. I don't think it's sick. I think it's . . . a *soaring* sensation. I have a sense of freedom, as if I'm no longer bound by the rules and restrictions of childhood. I can open locked boxes and break meaningless oaths with impunity. I'm on the verge of understanding mysteries that have been closed to me. I'm emerging from the old dark world of tunnels and terrors, and coming to a broad upland where the air's bright, and remote blue horizons open all around.

She holds out her hand for the cigarette and takes another little puff. This time it makes her laugh as well as choke.

'What?' I ask.

'Us,' she says, when she can speak. 'Smoking.'

We pass the magic fire back and forth. We hold it in various bold and striking ways – between two extended fingers, like Geoff, or with the flat of the hand raised up beside the face like a salutation, and the elbow supported in the other hand, like Mrs Sheldon. We push our lips forwards to receive the sacrament. We draw them in to savour the mouthful of smoke. We watch the little red glow brighten and fade with our breath, and the blue smoke curl up through the leaves.

We lie back in the dust and squint at the sky and smoke and talk about things. Or rather Barbara does. She hates Miss Pinnegar, the art teacher at her school – they all hate her, they call her Drawing Pin. Rosemary Winters used to be her best friend, but she isn't any more, because she said something spiteful to Ann Shakespeare about her. She wonders what Keith's mother and her boyfriend will do now that everyone's on the watchout for him.

'It's not her boyfriend,' I explain calmly. 'They're just German spies.' Only I don't, of course. I say nothing.

'Perhaps next time he comes in the middle of the night she'll creep out of the house and they'll run away together,' she whispers.

'They're German spies!' Only the reason I don't say it this time is because I know that it's all much more complicated than that. Softness and bosoms and kisses come into it somehow. Simple spying was part of the world of secret passages and bayonets that has just curled away with the blue smoke of the cigarette, and dispersed in the open sky.

She takes another puff of the cigarette and hands it to me. There's almost nothing left but the cork tip.

'We could watch to see what happens,' she says softly. 'We could creep out of our houses at night and hide in here, like your brother and Deirdre.'

A kind of shiver goes through me, and an uneasiness stirs in my stomach. Perhaps I am beginning to feel sick. What I've remembered, as I think about me and Barbara hiding here side by side in the night, is that in three days' time it will be the dark of the moon.

I've remembered something else, too – where I last saw a packet of cork-tipped cigarettes.

Perhaps it wasn't Geoff and Deirdre in here last night. Perhaps it was him. Watching the house. Waiting his moment . . .

The cork-tipped cigarettes in the hidden box beyond the tunnel were Craven A. I look at the stub I'm holding. The name on the paper has been smoked away. Between us we've destroyed the evidence.

And now everything has changed once again. The air of the Close each evening is full of birdsong – I've never really noticed it before. Full of birdsong and summer perfumes, full of strange glimpses and intimations just out of the corner of my eye, of longings and sadnesses and undefined hopes.

It has a name, this sweet disturbance. Its name is Lamorna.

Lamorna. I find the word on my tongue over and over again, saying itself of its own accord. Lamorna is the softness of Barbara Berrill's dress as she leaned across me to look in the trunk. Lamorna is the correct scientific description of the contrast between the bobbly texture of her purse and the smooth shininess of its button. Lamorna is the indoor-firework smell of the match, and its two shining reflections in her eyes.

But Lamorna is also the name of the softness in Keith's mother's voice when she called to me through the leaves, wanting my help, and the pleading look I glimpsed for a moment in her eyes before she realised I wasn't alone.

Lamorna. A distant land across the sea, blue on the blue horizon. The sighing of the trees. The name of a song I once heard. There's just a little of the terror of the Lanes in it, too, and the silence under the elders.

Lamorna . . . And there it is, the word itself, picked out in raised metal letters, painted over in the same peeling colour as the woodwork behind them, almost hidden by a wild profusion of dog-roses, on the front gate of Barbara Berrill's house.

On one side of the street, stiffly and correctly engraved among the verdigris beyond the standard roses: *Chollerton*. On the other, in those carefree, open-hearted, peeling metal letters: *Lamorna*.

I see all kinds of things I never saw before, wherever I look, now that the lamorna's in the air. I look up at the evening sky, as Keith's mother did as she stood patiently at her garden gate, waiting to be escorted to the letter box, and I see to my surprise that it's not emptiness she was looking at, not a serene eventlessness at all, but something infinitely complex. There's a silent air battle going on up there – the great evening dogfight between the high-flying insects and the low-flying swallows.

And once again, ten thousand feet beyond the swallows, I see the heroic vapour trails I saw scribbled across an earlier summer sky. Now it's night, and I hear the sirens starting up near and far, treading on each other's heels, and the heavy throb of the bombers. I see the searchlights fingering the universe, and the high palace of the falling flares, and the flickering orange above Miss Durrant's house.

And suddenly, in a series of brief tableaux, as if the darkness were being lit up by the flashes of unheard bombs, I see the whole story.

The ghostly, silent shape of the parachute floating down, once again . . . The sudden sickening impact of the ground . . . The man lies there stunned, then crawls over the incomprehensible dark landscape of this enemy land, over the inexplicable pattern of cracked soil and coarse clumps of vegetation, of abandoned kerbstones and overgrown manholes, looking for a refuge . . .

He's not a spy at all. He's not an old tramp. He's a German airman who has been shot down.

Somehow Keith's mother found him. In the blackout one night, perhaps, as he crept out on this side of the tunnel looking for food. She felt sorry for him. She remembered the silver-framed portrait she has at home of another airman who may also fall to earth one night in an alien land, and crawl into a hole in the ground for refuge, and need help. She said nothing to anyone. Only to Auntie Dee, under the picture of that same other airman. She began to collect food and cigarettes from Auntie Dee's house, and leave them out for him . . . Clean clothes . . . Hot coffee to fill the thermos she has taken from the picnic basket . . . Then two small boys find the box where the things are left. Now she has to bring everything to his hiding place instead. She has to meet him face to face. Every day she comes . . . And gradually she takes him to her bosom . . .

I feel light-headed. With relief that Keith's mother is not a spy after all. With alarm that she's giving aid and comfort to the enemy, even so, because a shot-down German airman's still a German. And with some generalised excitement that flickers in the air, as shifting and unlocatable as summer lightning. It's something to do with that bosom she's taken him to. I can feel the disturbing softness of it when I collided with her in the tunnel. It mingles with the softness of Barbara Berrill's dress, as she leaned across me to look in the trunk . . .

Its name breathes itself through the perfumed air as slowly and softly as a sigh:

L . . . a . . . m . . . o . . . r . . . n . . . a . . .

But something has changed about the perfume of the air in the lookout. The guileless sweetness of the limes and the honeysuckle has been overlaid by a sweetness of a different kind, harsh, coarse, and reckless, with just a touch of the catty stink of elder in it.

The source of it turns out to be very close to hand as soon as I lift my eyes and look. The dull green branches of the bushes that I'm hiding beneath are beginning to dissolve into a sea of reeking white.

Amidst the white, one warm afternoon, I find two brown eyes watching me. My heart jumps, first with excitement and then in the next instant, as I realise who it is, with anxiety.

'Stephen,' says Keith's mother quietly, 'now you're alone . . . I want to ask you to do something for me. May I come in?'

9

I stop for a moment again in front of Meadowhurst. There's Stephen, the second tub of geraniums from the left. And there *she* is, Keith's mother, crouching beside him, the third tub.

The game has entered a new phase altogether. I think Stephen understood this even as she settled herself in front of him. In fact it had completely turned around. He'd begun as her antagonist, and now he was to become her accomplice.

She'd changed in some way. I remember noticing that at once, too. She'd changed as much as the bushes had, as much as Stephen himself, and everything else around him.

What was the change? I think she seemed somehow even more perfect than before. Her lips were redder, her cheeks smoother, her eyes more lustrous. She had a pale blue silk cravat around her neck, high under her chin, and fastened in front with a silver clasp. It seemed to lift her head, and to give her an air of regal haughtiness, even as she sat cross-legged in the dust in front of Stephen like a beggar. Which I suppose she'd become. Only now do I realise to quite what extremity she must have been driven to humble herself in this way, and to ask a child for help.

What I find it difficult to remember now is how she ever managed to broach the subject. I think she simply put the shopping basket she was carrying on the ground between them. I think she told him very quietly that he must know what she wanted him to do. I don't suppose he responded to this. But of course he did understand.

I think she apologised for having to ask him. I think she told him that she couldn't see any other way – that there was no one else she could turn to.

Did she explain why she couldn't ask Keith? She didn't need to – Stephen understood perfectly well. Keith didn't know about any of this – he'd chosen not to. In any case there was something unthinkable about the very idea of her asking him to do it. What exactly was this unthinkable something? – Nothing exactly. What's unthinkable can't in its nature be exactly anything. Its inexactitude is what makes it so overpowering. It pervades the air unseen, like a perfume.

The contents of the basket were covered with a clean teacloth, as if it were a picnic the two of them were going to share. She didn't show them to him. I think she explained that they were simply a few little things he needed. That who needed? He. I think that was what she called him. He . . . him . . .

Whoever and whatever he was or wasn't, Stephen was still quite clear about one thing: he was a German. There was no way round that.

He didn't have a ration book, she told Stephen. He was ill – he really needed a doctor. She mentioned the damp. She didn't specify where the damp was.

Stephen remembered that quiet, persistent coughing from the underground chamber beneath the elders. He also thought of the German sitting where he was sitting then, in the lookout, lighting a cigarette in the darkness, and coughing, and stubbing it out again unsmoked.

She would have liked to send him something hot, she said, and of course Stephen knew why she couldn't: because the thermos flask was back in the picnic basket on the garage wall, and would stay there for the Duration.

She told Stephen not to go down the steps, but to leave everything on the ground outside – just to call out and tell him it was there.

'You do know where to go, don't you?' she asked Stephen quietly. 'I haven't just imagined that?'

Stephen kept his eyes on the ground and said nothing. She understood, though. He did know. She hadn't just imagined it.

* * *

'So will you do it for me, Stephen?'

Still I keep my eyes on the ground. I feel the soft, silent fall of the parachute in the darkness. I feel the bone-breaking impact, the slime of blood on the hands . . .

He's a German, though!

'Stephen, darling, listen,' she says, as softly as the silken rustle of the parachute. 'I can't explain. It would take too long, and I've got to get back, and anyway there are some things that are not terribly easy to explain to other people.'

The softness of her voice, her closeness as she leans towards me, and above all the 'darling' that she uses for her own son, make my face dissolve, I know, like the canopy of the parachute settling on the ground around me. But he's a *German*!

'Anyway, I think you *do* understand,' she says, as softly as before. 'Don't you, Stephen? In a way? You understand that sometimes people find themselves isolated. They feel that they're outcasts, that everyone's against them. You've seen boys at school being picked on for one reason or another. Perhaps because of something that they can't help at all – something about the way they look, or the way they talk, or because they're not very good at games. Or even because of nothing at all. Just because they're who they are. Yes?'

I nod. I do know a boy who has been picked on. I can feel the pain in my ears, and the fear that they're going to come right off in my tormentor's hands as my head's rocked back and forth. But then I'm not a *German*! That makes it quite different!

'So *will* you, Stephen? Will you do it?'

Time is pressing her. I've no idea where Keith's father is or what he's doing, but she knows that it can't be long now before he notices her absence. Suddenly all the urgent confidence that she came with ebbs out of her voice.

'I know how terrible it is to have to ask you, Stephen. I shouldn't do it if I could think of any other way. I feel so . . .'

The words stop. I look up to see what's happened. Her hands are pressed to her mouth, and her eyes are filling with tears. Two almost inaudible words finally escape through her fingers: 'So ashamed.'

She's going to cry. I look away. This is the worst thing of all. I shall never be able to hold out now. But I *must*! He's an outcast for good reason – because he's *German*! I make one last final effort.

'Auntie Dee,' I say. 'She could take the things. You could look after Milly, and Auntie Dee could take them.'

Silence. I look up again. She's absolutely motionless, hands still pressed to her mouth, gazing at me through the brimming tears. And all at once I understand. The man who once used to come visiting Auntie Dee in the blackout is the same man as the German in the Barns. It's so obvious now I've thought of it. It was Auntie Dee, not Keith's mother, who found him. It was Auntie Dee who first took him to her bosom.

Keith's mother gives a terrible, shuddering sob. Then another and another.

Silence again. I sneak another look. She's sitting with her head bent, her hands covering her face entirely, silently shaking. I look away again. I mustn't see her like this. Odd spots of wetness appear in the dust between us. One falls on the back of my hand.

I wait, scarcely daring to breathe. On the opposite pavement the Geest twins are chalking out a hopscotch diagram, and Norman Stott is rubbing it out again with the sole of his shoe. Barbara Berrill walks past, calling out to the Stotts' dog. At any moment one of the children is going to hear, or Barbara's going to come back and look in through the leaves. I remember her sitting where Keith's mother's sitting now, her eyes also full of tears from the smoke of the cigarette, and I realise that the very things that seemed so simple and straightforward then are not simple and straightforward at all, but infinitely complex and painful.

Still the silent shaking goes on. And it's all my fault. It's because I found the box, so that Keith's mother had to take Auntie Dee's messages all the way to the Barns instead. It's because she had to start meeting the German face to face. She's taken him to *her* bosom – and taken him away from Auntie Dee's. This is why she can't ask Auntie Dee to go. This is why she never goes to Auntie Dee's house any more. Just by looking at things I shouldn't have looked at, I've changed them. I've set Keith's mother and father against each other. I've set Keith's mother and Auntie Dee against each other. I've ruined everything. 'I'm sorry,' I mutter, 'I'm sorry.'

Keith's father emerges from their back yard. He crosses the front garden, whistling the tune that never reaches its destination, and looks round the other side of the house, then comes to the front gate and stands looking down the road. The whistling trails away.

Keith's mother sighs a long, slow sigh. She's stopped crying. She's watching Keith's father through her fingers. He turns uncertainly, and goes back towards the kitchen door.

'I must go,' she says in a little voice that only just manages to escape from her throat. She pulls a handkerchief out of her sleeve, and dabs it to her eyes. 'I'll just tidy myself up a little first, perhaps.'

I look at her. She's completely changed once again. All that perfection she arrived with has become blurred, and I realise why it had seemed so particularly vivid before: she'd made herself up even more thoroughly than usual.

'I'm most awfully sorry, Stephen,' she says. 'Let's just pretend all this never happened, shall we? I know how good you are at pretending. And don't worry about the things. I'll somehow think of some other way to do it. I should never have asked you. That was quite wrong. I just felt so . . . so *helpless* . . .'

She holds the handkerchief to her mouth and gazes thoughtfully past me for a long time, as if she's remembering something in the remote past.

'Yes, that's what we used to do,' she says dreamily. 'I used to look after Milly while Dee went.'

I can scarcely recognise her now she's wiped most of the make-up off her face. But there's also something curiously familiar about her appearance from some other context altogether, as if I've seen her before in a dream.

'Oh, Stephen,' she says. 'Life can be so cruel sometimes. It all seems so easy for a start. And then . . .'

She puts her arms round her knees, the way Barbara does, and rests her chin on them.

'When you and Keith started your little game of detectives,' she says, 'when you began looking in my things and following me around, I don't suppose it ever occurred to you that it would all end up like this, with me crying on your shoulder. Poor Stephen! It was a naughty thing to do, you know, spying on people. All the same, what a terrible punishment!'

She gives me a wan smile. I know now where I've seen that face. It's the one that looks seriously out of the silver frame in her sitting room. It's the face of the young girl wearing long gloves and a broad-brimmed hat who's playing at being a grown-up, with a protective arm around the little sister who's playing at being a child and smiling so trustingly up at her.

Once again I feel the locked box beginning to open and reveal its mysteries. I'm leaving behind the old tunnels and terrors of childhood – and stepping into a new world of even darker tunnels and more elusive terrors.

She touches her fingers against her cheeks and eyes. 'Oh dear,' she says, 'I haven't even got a mirror with me. Am I a complete mess?'

I suppose she is. I shake my head.

She picks up the basket to go. Keith's father appears silently from the far side of the house. Once again he comes to the garden gate and gazes silently down the street. She waits.

'Never mind,' she says, 'I'll think of something. You won't tell anyone, Stephen, will you, now you know who it is?'

I shake my head. And I reach over and take the basket out of her hand.

She gazes at me in surprise. 'Oh Stephen,' she whispers. 'Really?'

She leans forward and kisses me. I duck awkwardly away, and her lips catch me on my eyebrow. But I can feel on my forehead the tears running down her cheeks again.

As Keith's father waits at the front gate he resumes his whistling, abstractedly, inconclusively. He goes back to the house, still whistling. Keith's mother clambers out along the passageway. I try not to imagine what will happen when she reaches home.

She stops again, looks at the cloud of white blossom around her head, and wrinkles her nose.

'You see?' she says. 'I told you it was going to be absolutely overpowering.'

She was right – it is. Or at any rate its sweet reek has overpowered me.

And, woven somehow into the sweetness of the smell, like the words into the music of a song, is the lingering sweetness of the sound:

$$L \ldots a \ldots m \ldots o \ldots r \ldots n \ldots a \ldots$$

I push the basket away behind me, to make it as inconspicuous as possible. But Barbara still can't take her eyes off it. She sits cross-legged in the dust, exactly where Keith's mother sat, leaning sideways to see past me.

'What does she want you to do with it?' she asks.

'Nothing.'

'What did she say?'

'Nothing. I don't know.'

'She just left it here and didn't say anything about it?'

'I can't remember.'

Barbara smiles, but it's not the little conspiratorial smile she smiled the last time we met. It's her big smile again, her big mocking smile. I should have gone at once, as soon as Keith's mother left. I was just waiting while I thought about it, to make sure I was ready to go through the Lanes again, past the dogs, to the dark stairway down into the earth under the elders.

'She was crying,' says Barbara softly.

There's something intimately shameful about this accusation. I'm ashamed on Keith's mother's behalf, and on my own for having witnessed her tears. 'She wasn't crying,' I say.

'Yes, she was. I was watching you both. You didn't know, did you?'

'Of course I knew.'

'No, you didn't.'

My heart sinks. How have we got back to all this stupid did/didn't, now that we've left childish things behind? How can the sunlit world have become so suddenly dark?

Barbara's mocking smile is meaner than ever. 'She kept dabbing her eyes. And her make-up went all funny.'

'She was laughing,' I say hopelessly.

'Laughing?' Barbara's mocking smile becomes larger than ever. 'What was she laughing about?'

'Nothing.'

'She was laughing about nothing? Why, is she a loony, then, like Eddie Stott?'

What's happening? I've never heard her say things like this before. Not since the Lamorna time began.

She goes on looking at the basket. Her curiosity outweighs her meanness. 'I could come with you,' she says in a more friendly voice. 'I could help you take it.'

I'd like to respond to this, but I don't see how I can. I shake my head miserably. She looks away, rebuffed. 'Oh, well, do it yourself, then. I don't care.'

I sit there looking at the ground. I almost had my courage up before she arrived. I was almost ready to face the dogs in the Lanes, even to get close to the German.

'Off you go!' she taunts.

I can feel the courage ebbing out of me again with every word she speaks.

'I'm not going to *follow* you! Is that what you're worried about? Why should I care where you take her stupid things?'

Impasse. We're going to be here for ever.

'What's inside it, anyway?' she asks finally, her dismissive tone softened a little once again by her curiosity.

I shrug. 'Just some things.'

'What things?'

'I don't know. *Things.*'

'Secret things? Like in your box? Rusty old carving knives?'

I'm too miserable to speak, even if I could think what to say.

She suddenly giggles. 'Or are *you* her boyfriend?' she says softly. 'That would be funny, if your best friend's Mummy was your girlfriend!'

And now I think I recognise something in her mocking smile, some small glint of sadness, that's almost like the pleading look in Keith's mother's eye when she read me her lecture about the little privacies that people might wish to protect. At that hint all my anguish comes bursting out. 'I thought', I cry, 'that we were going to be . . .'

But there I stop. *What* did I think we were going to be? I was going to say 'friends'. Isn't that what she said before, that I could be her next-best friend after some girl at school? And then didn't she say that she and the girl at school weren't best friends any more? I hesitate to mention the word 'friends', though, because she's started all this talk about people's girlfriends and boyfriends again, and I don't mean anything silly and horrible like that.

Still, no other word presents itself. 'Friends,' I say wretchedly. 'I thought we were going to be friends.'

And just as suddenly as the trouble started, it finishes. Her big mocking smile vanishes. She gives me one of her little smiles instead. She really wants to be friends just as much as I do.

She unpops her bobbly blue purse. '*I've* got something secret to show *you*,' she says. She holds out the open purse, and we both look into it, our heads next to each other, the curled-up end of her hair brushing my cheek. Among the ha'pennies and threepenny bits is a packet, bent and flattened by the narrowness of the purse, with the words '10 Players Navy Cut' along the edge.

We move our heads apart and look at each other. 'I took it out of Deirdre's satchel,' she says.

Inside the packet is a single cigarette, bent and flattened like the packet itself. She pops the purse shut again. The popper opens and closes with a sweetly satisfying sound, I notice, as if it were saying 'Lamorna' as a single syllable. 'That's why I was coming to your camp,' she says. 'I thought we could have another smoke together.'

The air's full of sweetness and birdsong again. I shrug offhandedly to conceal the great leap of excitement inside me. 'All right,' I say grudgingly.

I fetch the matches from the trunk. She puts the cigarette in her mouth, then glances slyly at me as I light it for her. I see the little spark of reflected flame in each of her pupils, and I know that now I'll have to let her see my secret in return. She lifts her head and releases a mouthful of smoke. She hands the cigarette to me, and even as I draw upon it she leans across me and pulls the teacloth up from the basket. I make no move to stop her. Our quarrel has apparently ended in perfect agreement.

From underneath the teacloth she takes out two eggs. She holds them up for me to see, grinning. I nod. She puts them carefully aside. I hand her the cigarette and she draws on it while I reach into the basket in my turn, and take out a small packet wrapped in greaseproof paper. Inside it are two rashers of bacon.

Barbara giggles. 'I thought it was going to be things for them to have a midnight feast with. Sweets and beer and things.'

She brings out a handful of potatoes and carrots. I bring out a tin of Spam and a piece of corned beef.

'Funny sort of midnight feast,' says Barbara.

I feel in the basket again and find a little white box. On the label is a familiar printed heading: 'W. Walworth Watkins, MPS FSMC FBOA, Dispensing Chemist and Optician.' Underneath the heading is a handwritten inscription: 'Master K. R. G.

Hayward. M & B tablets. One to be taken with water three times a day.'

'M & B,' says Barbara. 'It's what you have when you've got a temperature.'

I know. I've had them myself. These are probably left over from some illness Keith had last winter.

Barbara takes another drag on the cigarette, and feels in the basket again. This time she brings out an envelope. It's sealed, but there's no address on it – not even an x. She looks at me, with her little conspiratorial smile.

I take it out of her hands. We're not going to look inside a private letter. Looking at the marks on a blotter is one thing, because they've been left around for anyone to see, but actually opening the envelope is quite different. Everyone knows that.

She sits watching me reflectively, letting the smoke gradually escape from her mouth. Then she leans slowly forward until her face is only a few inches from mine.

'What?' I ask apprehensively, starting back, though I can guess.

She leans closer still, and rests her lips against mine.

Some moments go by. She takes her lips away.

'Was that nice?' she asks.

Nice? I hadn't really got round to thinking about whether it was nice or not. I was too busy thinking about the germs.

'Deirdre said it was nice,' she says.

She leans forward again. I close my eyes, but this time I manage not to flinch. I'm aware of a fleck of tobacco on her lower lip, and of not being quite sure where the burning end of the cigarette has got to. An odd thought comes into my head: that I've found a value for x.

Again she takes her lips away and looks at me. 'Well?'

'Quite nice,' I say politely.

She straddles across me, pushing me back on to the ground. What she's doing is leaning over to take the bayonet out of the trunk. She slips the letter out of my fingers, and slits it open.

'No!' I say urgently. 'No, no, no!'

I struggle to sit up, but I'm helpless underneath her. She smiles triumphantly down at me, and slides the letter out of the envelope.

'No!' I cry, thrashing about like a beached fish. 'Don't! We mustn't, we mustn't!'

I realise that someone's peering in at us through the leaves.

'Can I have a word with you, old chap?' says a terrifyingly familiar voice.

Keith's father. Here of all places. Now of all times.

He stands waiting in the street while Barbara gets quietly off me. We don't look at each other. Keith's father, I can see, also has his eyes averted. Barbara begins to put everything back into the basket. I crawl out into the open, and stand in front of him, awaiting my fate. He glances briefly at me.

'Bring the basket,' he says shortly, and waits while I go back and take it out of Barbara's hands. 'Don't give it to him!' she whispers, letting it go as helplessly as I'm taking it. 'You mustn't let him have it!'

I follow him across the street to the Haywards' house, holding the basket with both hands, sick with apprehension. It's the first time he's ever addressed me direct. And he called me 'old chap', almost as if I were one of the family.

I'm not going to give him the basket, though. By the time he leads the way into the side door of the garage I've recovered from my surprise sufficiently to be absolutely certain about that.

I don't know how I'm going to manage it, but I'm not going to hand it over, whatever happens.

Not even if he calls me 'old bean'.

The light's on above the workbench, and he bends over some small piece of metal held in the jaws of the great vice. He puts his head down very close to the work, still whistling. He seems to be measuring whatever it is with a micrometer. The air's full of the smell of sawdust and oil, of concrete and car, and of fear.

Without warning he stops whistling. 'Word of advice, old fellow,' he says. 'Silly games. Don't play them.'

Silence. He loosens the micrometer, and tightens it on another part of the metal. I watch him, hypnotised, with no idea what to say or do.

'Silly games of let's-pretend,' he continues, bending to read the micrometer. 'Somebody asks you to play a silly game of let's-pretend, tell them, "No, thank you very much – I'm not such a fool." Child, grown-up – makes no difference. Tell them, "No, thanks. Nothing doing."'

He suddenly looks up sharply at me, smiling his thin smile. 'Yes?' he demands. I nod mutely. He goes on looking at me. 'People make awful asses of themselves with let's-pretend, you see, old chap. Get themselves in no end of a muddle. I've had a word with Keith. I don't want any more ideas put in his head.'

He smiles his terrible smile again, but this time I see just the slightest hint in it of what I saw in Keith's mother's smile. It comes to me that he finds this conversation as difficult as I do, and for a moment I glimpse a more general and more surprising truth – that adults are not after all members of some completely different species from myself. Even Keith's father belongs to a branch of the animal kingdom that has some kinship with my own.

'So – game over. Yes?'

I nod again. There's nothing else I can do.

'Basket, then.'

The basket. We've got there.

I look at the floor. Silence. The surface of the concrete is more complex than you might imagine. There are pebbles of different sizes embedded in it. Some of the pebbles have somehow freed themselves and disappeared, leaving little pebble-shaped craters.

'Basket. On the bench, old chap.'

I go on looking at the floor. In some of the craters, I see, smaller pebbles have taken refuge, like hermit crabs in abandoned snail shells.

'I'm not going to say it again, old bean.'

Still nothing happens, though. Slowly another revelation begins to form, even in the midst of my fear: he's doing nothing because there's nothing he can do. He can't cane me, because by some improbable stroke of kindly providence he's not my father. He can't snatch the basket out of my hands, because it would be beneath his dignity to secure something by force and not by fear. All he can do is wait for me to submit.

And I won't.

This is the bravest and the most shocking thing I've done in my entire life. I can feel my limbs trembling with horror and exultation.

Still the silence goes on. I lift my eyes from the floor and look at him. He lifts his eyes from his work and looks at me. For a moment we gaze at each other.

His smile has vanished. He doesn't seem to be angry, though. He seems to be baffled. He doesn't know what to do.

He also looks more wretched than I have ever seen anyone look before.

We both quickly look away.

'*Please*,' he says, in a strange, small, urgent voice.

And I give in. Against this shameless and terrible word I can't hold out. I put the basket next to the jaws of the great vice.

I know that this is the weakest and most cowardly thing I've done in my life. In the course of a single minute I've tumbled from best to worst. And even as I do it, I hear the unhurried, tranquil footsteps crossing the yard behind my back.

'Ted, darling,' says Keith's mother's voice, 'Keith *still* hasn't finished his maths, but he has been working on it for an hour and a half, poor lamb . . .'

She stops. 'Hello, Stephen,' she says in surprise. I can't look at her. There's a silence that seems to go on for ever, and I know what she's doing. She's looking at the basket on the workbench. Another eternity, and I know she's looking at me, then at Keith's father, then at the basket again.

At the disarranged teacloth that no longer hides its contents. At the egg that Barbara has broken in her haste. At the opened envelope.

'Oh, thank you,' she says calmly, and scarcely a moment has elapsed after all. 'Aren't those the things you and Keith borrowed for your camp?'

She goes over to the bench to pick up the basket. Keith's father silently moves it out of her reach, then bends over his work, smiling his smile.

Another eternity, and then she turns to me again. 'Why don't you go and find Keith and cheer him up?' she says calmly. She turns back to Keith's father. 'I think he might reasonably call it a day on the maths now, mightn't he?'

What happens after this I don't hear, because I'm already out of the door. Keith's waiting on the kitchen step on the other side of the yard, his maths homework in his hands. He looks at me, evidently too exhausted by his struggle with the maths, or too cowed by whatever's been going on in this house, to be surprised. I don't try to cheer him up, as his mother suggested. I don't say anything to him, because I'm too ashamed to speak.

I run back to the street. Barbara Berrill's lurking there, waiting for me, subdued and frightened. 'The basket,' she whispers, looking at my empty hands. 'He took the basket. What did he do? Did he cane you . . .?'

I can hardly hear what she's saying, though, because I'm already halfway down the street.

I'm running home to Mummy. My life's over.

'I can't do anything', says my mother for the tenth time, 'if you don't tell me what the matter is.'

'*Nothing*'s the matter,' I insist miserably, also for the tenth time.

'But I can *see* you've been crying. Look at you!'

'I *haven't* been crying!'

'Is it something at school? You're not worrying about the exams? The other boys aren't saying things about you again? They're not calling you those names?'

'No.'

'Have you and Keith fallen out?'

'No!'

Even my father's aware that something's wrong. He sits me down in the armchair opposite him after dinner, and gazes at me with mournful sympathy. 'I'd take all your troubles from you if I could,' he says, 'and give you mine instead. You've got worse troubles than anyone's ever had before, I know that. Mine you wouldn't find so bad. Other people's troubles never are.'

My father has troubles? If anything could make me smile, this would. What would my father have troubles about? *He* hasn't betrayed his country. *He* hasn't been given a task and failed, or been entrusted with a secret and revealed it, or left a sick and starving man to die. *He* hasn't been tormented by that rank sweetness in his nostrils and that soft music of Lamorna in his ears, and lost them both.

'But then yesterday's troubles aren't as bad as today's troubles,' he says. 'And when you wake up in the morning yesterday's troubles are what today's troubles will be.'

Very possibly, but the difficulty is getting to tomorrow. How do you wake up in the morning if you've never been to sleep? Long after Geoff's finally hidden his stack of old naturist magazines away under his bed and turned off his torch, I'm still wide awake. I hear the last trains of the day passing behind the houses on the other side of the street, bursting out of the embankment and rattling down the gradient, or straining up it in the opposite direction, and I live through the long intervals between them. I get up and put my head under the blackout blind. In the gap between the Sheldons' house and the Stotts' a last thin smile of moon is lingering above the sunset, as if Keith's father had just passed that way. It's changed sides since I last saw it, as I seem to have done. It's become the converse of itself. Its arms are held out to the north instead of the south, and in them the last lingering shadow of the full moon I saw a fortnight ago lies dying.

By tomorrow night it will have been extinguished completely.

Nothing can happen in that darkness now, though. Can it? I go back to bed and watch the dim spill of twilight fade around the edges of the blind. Far on into the night, when no normal trains run, a steam locomotive labours slowly past, and the low rumble of its loaded trucks goes on and on, long after the locomotive itself has moved on into other people's dreams.

My troubles are getting not better but worse. Everything's getting more and more confused inside my head. I'm haunted by the dark figure who's simultaneously falling through the moonless night and lying on the bare earth in a strange country, dying of cold and hunger. All around him, mocking his loneliness, is the sweet reek of some intangible happiness, and the faint, melancholy notes of an old sad song called 'Lamorna'.

I must have been asleep after all, because I'm suddenly awake and full of a new anguish: he was dying down there in the damp subterranean gloom, and Keith's mother was nursing him, her bright arms round the fading ghost, even as Keith and I were hammering on the corrugated iron above his head.

I get up and creep into my parents' bedroom on the other side of the landing, as I used to if I had a nightmare when I was little. The room's full of their familiar breathing – the heavy, uneven sound of it and its stale bedroom smell. 'I had a bad dream,' I whisper pathetically, as I used to. They breathe on, oblivious. I get on to the bottom of the bed and cautiously make my way up until I can edge myself under the covers and insinuate myself into the narrow canyon between their backs. I've become a child again.

But now the old safe place is no longer the comfort it was. The walls of flesh on either side of me are claustrophobic. My parents' absorption in sleep merely makes me more distressingly aware of my own isolation in the world. I lie there more awake than ever, or more confused about whether I'm awake or not. Now the dying man's not him but me. It comes to me with a terrible force that one day I'm going to be lying in my coffin, deep in the earth. This very body of mine that's lying here tormented in the darkness will become lifeless stuff, held tight between the narrow wooden walls on either side, trapped by the lid pressing down on my chest and face. I understand fully for the first time that sooner or later there will come a day when I'm dead, and from that day forth I shall be dead for ever. I feel the blind terror sweep through me. I scream and scream, but no sound emerges, because I'm dead and deep below the earth. For ever.

Sudden light, too bright for me to open my eyes properly. Through my tears I can just glimpse my mother and father bending over me in hurriedly-woken consternation.

'What *is* it, love?' cries my mother. 'You *must* tell us what it is!'

I weep on, still unable to move between those narrow walls, still unable to explain – unable now to speak at all or even to shake my head.

My father's both wrong and right, I discover, when morning comes. My troubles are no less – but now at any rate I know what I have to do about them.

I have to make one more attempt to redeem all my failures – and this time I have to succeed.

I have to go down into the darkness and bring the dying man the help he's depending upon. I feel a sick dread at the prospect. The terrible dream I had in the night, if it was a dream, is with me still all through the day at school. We've got the English Composition exam, and I waste half the time gazing blindly at the paper in front of me, unable to decide whether to write about The Englishman's Home is His Castle or The Pleasures of Idling, because all I can think about is that other exam I have to sit after school, when I go down into the living grave.

At least there's no choice left to be made in this particular paper. I go straight to the bathroom cabinet as soon as I get home and find the box of pills I was prescribed last winter. I look in the cupboard under the stairs, where Geoff and I slept during the worst of the raids, and find, balanced on top of the electricity meters and fuse boxes, the random collection of packets and tins that my mother left there as emergency rations, along with the family first-aid box, in case the house was hit and we were trapped under the debris like Miss Durrant. I take a tin of pilchards and one of condensed milk, a packet of cheese biscuits and one of dried egg. We haven't slept under the stairs for a long time, and in any case it's difficult to know what my mother thought Geoff and I might do in here with dried egg.

I put all the provisions in my school satchel. What I can't find any substitute for, of course, is whatever was inside the envelope. I shall have to try to explain what's happened. Will he understand any English? How did he and Keith's mother communicate? If she's a German spy she presumably speaks German. I try to imagine her uttering those notorious gutturals . . . But she *isn't* a German spy! Is she? That all belongs to a past I've long since left behind. Haven't I?

'I'm going out to play,' I tell my mother.

She searches my face. 'With Keith?' she asks distrustfully.

'No.'

'Stand up for yourself,' she says. 'Don't let him be nasty to you.'

And once again I set out on that horrible journey. It's even more frightening now I'm on my own, of course, and the uncertainty at the end of it seems even more profound now that it's darkened by the lingering shadow of my dream.

The lake in the tunnel has shrunk in the dry midsummer weather to a chain of puddles. The hedgerows in the Lanes beyond have lost their damp, green freshness, and gone grey in the drifted dust. It's hot again, as it was when I came along here with Keith, and the air's very still. But this time there's an uneasy yellow light in the sky, and an occasional rumbling murmur that might be either thunder or a distant air raid.

One by one the disheartening landmarks are reached and left behind. The sycamore with the rotted rope. The little field of dock and sorrel. The nettle bed. The boot. The ruined armchair. Then comes the barking, and the dogs. Four of them today, and bolder now that I'm on my own, reeking of fear. Their rushes being them closer and closer to me, and one of them snaps at my hand. Two of them come at me from behind. In a panic I spin round to face them, and the swing of my satchel in their faces makes them jump back for a moment. I take it off my shoulder and whirl it round me. The children in front of the Cottages watch me as expressionlessly as before. One of them picks up a stone and throws it at me, and I flinch even in the middle of my struggles against the dogs. Moment by moment I'm expiating all the weakness I've shown.

A year goes by before I'm out of range of the children's gaze, and the last of the dogs has given one final bark and written me off.

Now the dried-up pond . . . the overgrown chalk pit . . . the green sea of weeds with the broken shafts of carts rising from it like spars from a sunken wreck . . . I walk more and more slowly, and stop. I've reached my destination.

The Barns, like everything else along the Lanes, are deeper in the rank midsummer green than they were before. The brick footings and the buckled sheets of corrugated iron are harder to make out.

I move reluctantly closer and stop again as I meet the sour, defeated smell of the elders. I begin to distinguish the brickwork, and the corrugated iron over the steps that lead down into the earth. There's no sign of life. I hold my breath and listen. Nothing. Only the occasional grumble of the distant thunder, and the small, offhand rattle of a passing train.

The living grave.

Then, among the smell of the elders, I catch the faint breath of the other smell I smelt before, of human excrement on freshly turned soil. There's still a living man here. And in the great silence that falls after the thunder quietens and the train pulls into the distant station beyond the tunnel, I hear the same sound as I heard before. A quiet, suppressed coughing.

Yes, he's here still, barely twenty feet away from me.

And now, of course, I don't know what to do. I think of Keith's mother, coming out of the world of silver ornaments and silver chimes and descending the great ladder of the world, rung by rung, until she finds herself where I'm standing, in the smell of the elders and the excrement – and then going on, further down, into the underworld.

I walk slowly forward to the head of the steps. The coughing stops. He's heard me.

The steps have crumbled and fallen away. At the bottom, under the corrugated iron, they vanish into darkness. In that darkness, I know, are his eyes, watching me.

I want to say some word to break the silence, but I can't think what that word should be.

I take out of my satchel the things I've brought, and put them down on the top step. I should be delivering something else too, I realise – some message to replace the letter I've lost. I should say something to explain why she hasn't come for so long, and why she'll never come again.

It's impossible, though. I've delivered all I can manage. I pick up my satchel to go, feeling his eyes on me.

And then, out of the darkness, his voice. A single quiet word: 'Stephen?'

10

Did Stephen understand at last who it was down there in the darkness, when he heard his own name spoken?

I really have no idea, as I try to piece all this together half a century later, whether he understood or not. All I can remember is the chill that went through him at the sound. All I can feel now is his frozen paralysis as he crouched there with his satchel half on his shoulder, unable to move, to speak, even to think at all.

'Stephen?'

Again, and as quietly as before. So it was someone who recognised Stephen. Someone who knew his name.

'What are you doing here?'

The voice was still quiet, but hard with alarm and suspicion. There was no trace of any foreign accent. He didn't sound like a tramp. From his voice he could almost have been a neighbour. A master at school. One of the family.

And Stephen still didn't know who it was?

I can't help wondering now what that figure in the darkness thought about this same question. I suppose he simply assumed that Stephen knew. I suppose it never even occurred to him that Stephen might *not* know. Certainly not that Stephen might both know and yet not know at the same time.

'Why have you come?'

Stephen managed to point at the things he'd put on the step.

'Was it Bobs who sent you?'

Bobs. The emergence of this name from the darkness was even more paralysing than the sound of his own, because he'd never heard anyone except Keith's father call her that before. He couldn't answer; he couldn't admit to knowing who Bobs was. Not when this intimacy was uttered by an old tramp. By a German. By an old tramp and a German with a voice almost as familiar as Keith's mother's own.

I remember that the coughing started again, and that Stephen plucked up courage to lift his eyes and look into the darkness, now that the darkness was melting a little. He could see a dark tangle of hair and beard, and the shaggy outline of it moving as the man coughed. For a moment Stephen glimpsed the brightness of the eyes watching him. The man was sitting on the ground, in what seemed to be a muddle of blankets and sacking, his back propped against the side of the underground chamber.

Did Stephen really not understand who it was? I think he still thought the man was an old tramp, but perhaps now he realised that he was also not an old tramp. I'm pretty sure he still adhered to the central tenet that the man was also a German. But perhaps he was beginning to understand that he was a German who was entirely English.

The coughing fit passes, and when the voice speaks again the tone's softer and less challenging. 'She can't come?'

I shake my head.

'Is there a letter. Have you brought a letter?'

Another shake. He sighs.

'Why can't she come?'

How can I ever begin to explain? 'She just can't.'

Another silence, and then the voice is softer still. 'Things are difficult for her?'

Again I don't respond. Again he understands my meaning. Again he sighs. 'What – Ted?'

I've heard Keith's mother say the word, just as I've heard him call her by her name. It's even more difficult to grasp, though, that Keith's father possesses such a simple human attribute as a name, and impossible to acknowledge it when it's uttered, as Keith's mother's was, as mine was, out of the alien darkness. I go on looking at the ground.

The man utters something that sounds like a little groan. 'I'm sorry,' he says, and the voice is softer still. 'Can you tell her that?'

Still no response from me, but this time he's not so sure what my silence means. 'Yes?' he persists. '*Will* you tell her?'

I nod, for the same reason as I've nodded on earlier occasions, because there's nothing else I can do, though how I'm ever going to tell her anything I can't imagine.

'And tell her . . .' He stops. 'Tell her . . .'

More coughing, and even when it ceases he still can't speak. I have the impression that he's begun to shiver. 'No, nothing else,' he says finally. 'It's over, then. It's over.'

Silence. I'm still crouching on the step, and my knees are cramped. Have I completed my task now? Have I explained everything I can manage to explain? Has he told me everything he can manage to tell me? Can I escape? The silence goes on and on. There seems to be nothing more that he wants to add. I stand up.

'Don't go,' he says at once, and there's that same note in his voice that I've heard before from Keith's parents – the command with the faint suggestion of pleading in it. 'Stay and talk for a moment. It gets a bit bleak, lying here. Nothing to see but that little patch of green at the top of the steps. Nothing to do but think. Funny view you get of the world . . . Sit down.'

I sit down on the top step, still helplessly obedient to adult authority.

'So why *you*?' he asks. 'Why did she pick *you*?'

I shrug. How can I explain?

'You seemed to be doing your level best to make a nuisance of yourself before. Shoving your nose into things that didn't concern you. That was just some kind of game, was it?'

I keep quiet. There's no way I can explain!

'So what's this? Another of your games? What did she tell you?'

'Nothing.'

'Nothing. But here you are.'

Once again I can't think of any response. Here I am, yes.

'So are you going to say anything to anyone else about it?'

Yes. No. I don't know what I'm going to do.

'Yes or no?' he persists.

I manage a shrug.

'What does *that* mean?'

'No,' I mumble.

I'm suddenly overcome by the sheer dreamlike strangeness of the situation. I'm negotiating with an old tramp. I'm being sworn to secrecy by a German. In a hole in the ground in the middle of a clump of elders, on a close summer afternoon with a hint of thunder in the air. And the strangest thing of all is that it's *not* strange. There's something absolutely ordinary about these elders, these broken bricks, this hole in the ground, this heavy day, this sick man.

'How's Milly?' he asks.

'All right,' I shrug.

He knows all our names. A cold unease goes down my spine to think that a German, an enemy who's fallen out of the night sky, speaks our language just as we do – that he knows all about us and our lives, just as if he were one of us. He's come and sat in our most secret places in the darkness, and watched us. He's moved invisibly amongst us all, like a ghost, and got to know our names and faces.

'What about . . .?' He stops. He seems to be trying to remember the name of someone else to ask after. '. . . Milly's mother?' he says finally. I make the same response.

His voice is so ordinary, so familiar. But he's not ordinary or familiar at all! He's an old tramp, filthy and bearded. And he's a *German*! His Germanness lingers in the air, as inherent a part of his identity as Mr Gort's murderousness, as intimately pervasive as the scent of the privet in my life, as insanitary as the germs he's giving off.

'I heard the dogs barking at you,' he says. 'Aren't you scared of them?'

Another shrug.

'So if I said, "Here, take this bucket, and go past the dogs, and fetch me some water from the well behind the Cottages . . ."?'

171

I nod. He makes no move to hand me a bucket, though.

He laughs. 'Yes, you'd go all right. You'd go like a shot. To get away from me. You'd go, but you wouldn't come back.'

I say nothing. He's said it for me.

'Poor kid,' he says, in a different voice. 'But that's what happens. You start playing some game, and you're the brave one, you're the great hero. But the game goes on and on, and it gets more and more frightening, and you get tired, because you can't go on being brave for ever. And then one night it happens. You're up there in the darkness five hundred miles from home and suddenly the darkness is inside you as well. In your head, in your stomach. You've cut out, like a dicky engine. You can't think, you can't move. You can't see, you can't hear. Everything's drowned by this great scream of terror in the darkness, and the scream goes on and on, and it's coming out of *you*.'

He's started to weep. Between one word and the next, out of nowhere. I long to be anywhere else on earth. But of course I have to wait.

'So then the others have to get you home,' he whispers. 'They're as sick at heart as you are, and somehow they have to keep their nerve and get you home. They trusted you and you failed them. And afterwards you could never look at them again, you could never be with them. From that day on you're an outcast. There's no place for you anywhere any more.'

He's shivering again, too, so that the weeping is trembly and strange. Gradually the fit subsides. 'So it's all over, is it?' he says, his voice steady again, but very low and flat. 'I always knew it would be, of course, sooner or later.'

Behind the trees a train emerges from the cutting.

'That's the only thing that keeps me sane,' he says. 'The sound of the trains. I lie here waiting for them. Three times an hour up, three times an hour down. Down to the houses in the Close. Up and out to the great wide world. I'm on all those trains. Down to the Close. Up and away.'

He starts to cough and shiver again.

'Off you go, then. Just pass me the things you brought.'

I can see the whiteness of his hand, held out in the darkness, waiting. There's nothing for it but to obey. I have to crouch to get under the corrugated iron, and I almost fall headlong on the broken steps into the pit below. I'm blocking out most of what little light there is, and the only thing I can make out is the smell. It's a mixture of damp earth, mildew, old sacking, mouldy food, illness, and the stale fustiness breathed out by the old men who drowse over the newspapers all day in the reading room of the public library.

I put the things on the ground beside him, still not looking at him, trying not to breathe in the germs. Out of the corner of my eye, though, as I turn to go, I'm aware of his two feverish eyes watching me from the dark tangle of hair and beard.

'Wait, wait!' he says.

I wait, my eyes now fixed longingly on the daylight at the top of the steps. I have to draw breath. I can feel the germs entering my body. Behind my back I hear the sound of a pencil scribbling over paper. A pause. Then the sound of the paper being torn off its pad and crumpled up. More scribbling. Again the paper's crumpled up and discarded.

He sighs. 'What's the use? I'd like her to have something from me, though . . .'

Silence. He seems to have forgotten about me. I start to move towards the steps.

'It was always her, you know,' he says quietly. I stop. 'From the very beginning. Always her.'

Another silence. Very quietly I make another attempt to leave.

'Wait!' he says again at once. 'Here. Take her this.'

I turn back, trying not to look at him directly. He's clawing at something wrapped around his neck. He folds whatever it is over and over, and holds it out. Reluctantly I reach towards him and take it. It's soft and silken, and hot from the fever of his body.

'Just so that she has something,' he whispers. 'And tell her . . . tell her . . . oh . . . nothing, nothing. Just give it to her. She'll understand.'

Already I'm out in the light, on the broken steps, grabbing my satchel, and stuffing the folded silken handful into it.

'Stephen!' he calls after me urgently as I start back towards the Lanes. 'Stephen! Tell her "for ever". Yes? "For ever".'

Low down in the sky, somewhere far away, summer lightning flickers. Ahead of me the dogs begin to bark at my approach.

For ever.

The three syllables echo softly on inside my head the way that Lamorna did before. Lamorna sounded like waves lapping softly on the shore; 'for ever' sounds like a key turning softly through the wards of a well-oiled lock.

'It's over,' he said. 'For ever.'

Something, I know, is being locked away into the past, the way Keith and I lock our secret possessions away inside the trunk, the way I shall be shut away myself one day inside my own narrow box. It's something which had always been so, as he said, from the very beginning. And I'm the one who has been chosen to turn the key. For ever. If I can just get that word to her, we can forget that any of this happened. Everything can be as it was before.

What will happen to *him*, down there in his grave under the elders? I don't know, I don't care. I don't have to bother about it, because whatever happens it will soon have happened, and then it will be in the past. For ever.

All night long the word revolves in my head with the seductive softness of the key turning in the padlock of our trunk. All through the geometry and French exams at school next day I feel the insidious softness of the little bundle of silk in my pocket. It's pale green, mottled with brown and veined with irregular black lines. It's some kind of map, and I can see from the one glance I've taken at it without unfolding it that the words on it are German: 'Chemnitz . . . Leipzig . . . Zwickau . . .' It's a map of his homeland – the last relic of his old life. I don't want to see any more, or to think about its naked Germanness. I simply want to give it to her, and turn the key through those three soft syllables.

The question is how. I can't just knock at the door. What should I do if it's Keith who answers it? Or if his father's within earshot?

All I can think to do is to go to the lookout and wait for an opportunity to present itself. She'll guess I've a message for her. She'll find some way to come across the road.

Even as I crawl into the lookout, though, I realise that it's changed. PRIVATE announces the tile inside the entrance. The floor has been swept clear of dead leaves and broken twigs. An old duster's been spread over the tin trunk, and in the middle of the duster is a jam jar with a bunch of wilting privet blossom.

At once I become conscious again of the rank sweetness in the air all round me, and my head fills with the soft murmur of Lamorna. A wave of excitement passes through me, to think of Barbara being in here on her own, setting her mark upon it. The wave of excitement is immediately succeeded by a wave of alarm and indignation at her presumption. I snatch the jar and the cloth off the trunk before Keith comes in and discovers them.

Gradually my alarm passes. Keith isn't going to come. All that part of my life's over, and there's no going back. I spread the cloth on the trunk again, replace the jar of privet, and begin my watch on the house. Something has changed there, too, I realise. Beside the front door, in the perfect order of the garden, is a piece of clutter, a foreign object that's never been there before: a pushchair.

At once I'm alarmed. In all the time I've been going to Keith's house I've never seen Auntie Dee or Milly there. I try to imagine Auntie Dee laughing her cheerful laugh among those reverent chimes and silences . . . or Milly hiding her sticky face in that discreet velvet upholstery . . .

Once again I hear the voice from the darkness beneath the earth, whispering my name. I close my mind to the memory. I don't have to think about these things, because soon they'll be gone for ever. All I have to do is wait, with my mind closed.

The front door opens, and Auntie Dee comes out carrying Milly. Milly's crying. Keith's mother appears in the doorway and stands watching, saying nothing, as Auntie Dee straps Milly into the pushchair. She goes on standing silently in the doorway as Auntie Dee hurries the pushchair towards the gate, then runs after her and says something to her. Auntie Dee stops and listens, her head bowed. Milly howls louder than ever. Keith's mother runs back to the front door. Auntie Dee runs after her. They stand talking on the step, while Milly howls by the gate. Dee presses her hands to her face, then to her ears.

Mrs Avery comes slowly up the street, carrying a heavy bag of potatoes. She crosses over to the Haywards and bends down to comfort Milly. Auntie Dee comes down the garden path, smiling at Mrs Avery. Keith's mother smiles from the doorstep.

Mrs Avery goes back across the street and continues towards her own house. Auntie Dee's smile vanishes. She picks up the weeping Milly, and half runs back down the street to her own house, her head down, scrambling the pushchair along in front of her.

Keith's mother comes irresolutely a few steps down the garden path, then realises she's being watched by Keith's father from the front door, and sets off to follow Auntie Dee down the street. Keith's father comes down to the front gate and examines the standard roses, whistling.

By the time Keith's mother reaches Auntie Dee's front door it's already shut. She knocks and waits. She knocks again. And waits. Keith's father goes back into the house, still whistling.

Keith's mother walks back up the road. Mrs McAfee is coming in the opposite direction. She smiles at Keith's mother. 'Your Ena Harkness is a real credit to the street!' she says. Keith's mother smiles back at her. 'Ted does work awfully hard at the garden,' she says. She walks up garden path, as calm and unhurried as ever. And as formally dressed, with another silk cravat, crimson this time instead of blue, high around her throat.

The front door closes. I feel the other piece of silk in my pocket, but it seems to me that I'm never going to be able to deliver my message now. Everything has changed once again, and changed for ever.

* * *

I'm wrong about Keith. When I crawl back into the lookout after supper, there he is, waiting for me.

He's sitting cross-legged in the middle of the newly swept floor, lost in his own thoughts. It must be at least two weeks since he was last in here, but he glances up at me as passingly as if it were a couple of hours. He offers no explanation either of why he's been making himself so scarce or why he's now reappeared. His face is set and brooding, intent upon the object he's fingering.

It's the bayonet.

The trunk's standing open. On the ground beside it are the duster that had been spread over the lid, the jam jar of privet blossom, and the tile marked PRIVATE.

Of course. I really knew all the time that he'd come back sooner or later. I feel the shame in my face, and then another and even more unpleasant sensation in my hands and throat and in the depths of my stomach. Fear.

I realise at once that there's one way, and only one way, in which I can avoid the punishment that's coming. I can show him the scarf. It's in the pocket of my shorts. This is why I've come back, to lock it away in the trunk.

I'll spread it out on the ground in front of him, and tell him that I've solved the problem he set us. I've unravelled the mystery that we began investigating together. I'll tell him quite simply? 'It's a secret message for your mother. From the old tramp in the Barns. He's a German. He's ill. Your mother has taken him to her bosom.'

I don't, though. I don't show him the scarf, because it can't be shown. I don't say the words, because they can't be said.

He raises his eyes from the bayonet and looks at me for the first time. His eyes are cold. 'You showed her our things,' he says softly.

'I didn't!' I cry. Too late I realise that he hasn't even named her, and that I shouldn't have let myself know who he meant.

He glances at the tile and the decorations he's removed from the top of the trunk.

'Yes, but I didn't show her anything inside it!' I cry. Because I *didn't*! She just looked. And in any case there's no way he can tell that the trunk has ever been opened.

He smiles his father's thin smile.

'I *didn't*!' I cry, almost weeping with sincerity. 'Honestly and truly!'

He begins to nod his head slightly, slowly and deliberately, as if he's counting off the seconds while he waits for my confession. 'You swore, old bean,' he says.

'I know, and I *didn't*!'

He suddenly raises the bayonet, and holds it in front of my face. He looks straight into my eyes, no longer smiling or nodding. 'Swear again,' he says.

I place my hand on the flat of the blade as I did before. And as I did before, I feel in my skin the electric sharpness that surrounds it. 'I swear,' I say.

'That I didn't break the solemn oath I swore never to reveal our secret things.'

I drop my eyes as I repeat the words. But I *didn't* break the oath! I *didn't* reveal our things!

'So help me God' I repeat after him, still not looking at him. 'Or cut my throat and hope to die.'

I manage to raise my eyes at last, and find that he's taking something out of the trunk and holding it up for me to see. It's the flattened Players cigarette packet. His eyes are still fixed on me. My face is burning with the heat of my shame.

'It wasn't . . . I didn't . . .' I stammer. 'She must have found the key.'

Suddenly his face is just in front of mine, though, smiling again, and I can feel the point of the bayonet against my throat. 'You swore,' he whispers. 'You double-swore.'

I can't speak. Something, either terror or the pressure of the blade on my windpipe, seems to be constricting my voice. I try to move my head back a little. The bayonet follows the movement, and presses harder.

'You said, "So help me God,"' he whispers. 'You said "Cut my throat and hope to die."'

I can't speak. I can't move. All I can do is to remain frozen with fear as the pressure of the blade against my windpipe gradually increases. He's not actually going to cut my throat, I understand that. He's going to go on until he breaks the skin, though, and lets the germs on the blade into my bloodstream. I can't take my eyes of that smile six inches in front of my face. It comes slowly closer and closer, as Barbara Berrill's face did when she kissed me. His eyes look into mine. They're the eyes of a stranger.

The blade presses slowly harder. And now suddenly I'm not sure after all that it *is* ever going to stop.

'And then you showed her,' he whispers. I know my eyes are filling with tears of pain and humiliation, and I can feel another little source of wetness around the point of the bayonet, as the blood wells out and mingles with the germs. And now I'm beginning to think it's true, that I did show her our secret things, though I suddenly wonder if it's really Barbara Berrill he means or if it isn't perhaps his mother. I have the odd idea that in some strange way we're talking about both of them – that the crime he's punishing in me is not mine at all, but one that's being committed inside his own house. And even in the extremity of my terror I suddenly realise where he learnt to practise this particular form of torture with this particular instrument, and why his mother, in the heat of summer, has taken to wearing that cravat pinned high around her neck.

Slowly, slowly the pressure on my throat increases. All I have to do is take out the scarf and give it him, as I gave his father the basket . . .

I can't do it, though. I can't let Keith's eye fall upon those rawly private words, sent on silk by that living ghost in the Barns to Keith's own mother. *Chemnitz . . . Leipzig . . . Zwickau . . .* They can't be revealed! For Keith's own sake as much as for hers. I can't show him what spying actually means – the fear, the tears, the silken, whispered words.

Chemnitz . . . Leipzig . . . Zwickau . . . If those names were ever spoken, another name might jump out after them, a name that would shame Keith for ever, a name that I've never allowed myself to think.

Now he's no longer smiling. His look's intent. The tip of his tongue's in the corner of his mouth, as it is when he's concentrating on some fine detail of a model he's building. The wetness on my throat begins to run down inside the front of my shirt. I become aware of a whimpering sound that must be coming from me.

And there we crouch, locked together by the logic of torture. We shall be here for ever. My hand would move and give him the scarf if it it could. But it can't. I gave in to his father. I'm not going to give in again.

And then it's over. The pressure on my throat begins to ease, and ceases altogether. I hadn't realised that my eyes had closed until I open them to see what's going on. Keith has sat back on his haunches again, and he's looking at the blood on the bayonet. He cleans it carefully in the earth.

'Do what you like, then, old bean,' he says coldly. 'Play houses with your girlfriend if you want to. I don't care.'

He looks at me with contempt.

'What are you blubbing about?' he says. 'That didn't hurt. If you think that hurt, you don't know what hurting is.'

I'm not crying, in fact. I have tears in my eyes and my breath is still coming in little convulsive gasps, but I'm not actually crying.

He shrugs. 'Anyway,' he says, 'it's all your own fault, old chum.' He rummages in the trunk and takes out a scrap of emery paper he keeps to shine the bayonet. He's evidently lost interest in me. My breathing gradually returns to normal. I'm still alive, and the harsh sweetness of the privet is back in my nostrils.

Neither of us says anything more. There's nothing more to say.

And the scarf is still in my pocket. He lost his nerve a fraction of a second before I lost mine. The world has changed yet again. And again, I think for ever.

I try to slip into the house without drawing attention to myself. I've done up the top button of my shirt, but it won't go as high as Keith's mother's cravat, and in any case I'm aware that the blood has splashed over the collar and started to make a dark patch below it. My plan is to get upstairs into the bathroom and put a plaster on my throat to stop the bleeding, then somehow to wash the shirt in the basin.

I'm already on the stairs when my mother emerges from the kitchen.

'Where on earth have you been?' she demands. 'What do you think you're playing at? Your satchel's still sitting exactly where you dumped it when you came in from school. You've got exams tomorrow! You've got revision to do!'

Before I can attempt to answer any of these questions, though, she's noticed the state of my shirt.

'What's *this*?' she says, even more crossly. 'Some kind of red stuff! It's not *paint*? Oh, Stephen, for heaven's *sake*! How do you expect me to get *paint* off? That's your school shirt!'

Suddenly she bends closer.

'Your neck . . .' she says. 'Your throat . . .'

She grabs me by the arm and marches me into the dining room, where my father's sitting at the table with his files and papers in front of him and his glasses on the end of his nose.

'Look!' she cries. 'Look what's happened now! I *knew* there was something wrong! You've got to put a stop to it!'

My father gently undoes my collar and examines my throat.

'Who did this to you, Stephen?'

I say nothing.

'It wasn't *Keith*?' demands my mother.

I shake my head.

'One of the other boys?'

I shake my head again.

My father leads me gently upstairs to the bathroom. 'I don't like bullying,' he says. 'I've seen too much of it in my lifetime.'

He fills the basin, then washes the wound with a tenderness that I can't remember in him before. My mother peels the bloody shirt off me. I rescue the scarf even as it falls to the floor, and crumple it tight in my hand.

Geoff emerges from our bedroom to find out what's going on, and stands watching from the bathroom doorway as the red threads curl away into the water like upside-down cigarette smoke.

'What happened, kid?' he asks. Calling people 'kid' is his latest affectation. 'Trying to cut your throat?'

'If it was Keith,' says my mother to my father, 'you'll have to say something to his parents.'

'This wasn't play,' says my father, gently swabbing. 'It almost went into his windpipe. It could have severed the artery.'

'You *must* tell us who it was, darling,' says my mother. 'It's not telling tales.'

I say nothing.

'He can't speak,' says Geoff. 'They've cut his vocal cords.'

'Keep out of this, will you, Geoff?' says my father. 'Just go and get the first-aid box from the cupboard under the stairs.'

He holds a piece of dry cotton wool to the wound, waiting for it to staunch. 'Just tell us what happened, Stephen.'

Silence.

'Was it one of the children? What did they say? Were they calling you names again? What names did they call you?'

Silence.

'Or was it a grown-up?'

Again I remain silent, and it occurs to me that I need never speak again.

'*Where* did it happen? In the street? Or at someone's house?'

'*Please*, darling,' says my mother. 'You might have been really badly hurt.'

'You could have been a goner, kid,' says Geoff, coming back with the first-aid box. 'Someone's swiped all the emergency rations, by the way.'

'Why can't you tell us what happened?' my father asks me, in his gentle, reasonable way. 'Did they tell you not to say anything? Did they threaten you?'

Silence.

'Stephen, what else happened? Did anything else happen?'

'Maybe it was that sexual deviant,' says Geoff. 'The one who's been hanging round at night.'

'Stephen,' says my father very slowly and carefully, 'there are some people in this world who get a kind of pleasure out of hurting others. Sometimes they like to hurt children. They do things to them that the children find frightening. If something like that has happened to you, then you must tell us.'

'He swiped the rations,' says Geoff. 'Then he slit Stevie's throat to keep him quiet.'

My father paints iodine on the wound. It stings far worse than it did when the bayonet went in. I wince and cry out. He takes a bandage out of the box and begins to wind it round my neck.

'Or was it *you* who took the rations, Stephen?' he asks very softly.

I weep silently with the pain.

'To play with in your camp?' pursues my father. 'Or perhaps to give to someone? Someone hanging around the street? Someone who asked you for food?'

'That old tramp, probably,' says Geoff.

'I'm not going to be angry, Stephen. It would have been a kind thing to do. I just have to know.'

'It's that old tramp who hides out in the Barns,' says Geoff.

'I thought they took him away?' says my mother. 'I thought they put him in prison after that little boy was interfered with?'

'Maybe he's back. Maybe he's the deviant.'

'Was it the tramp, Stephen?' asks my father.

I shake my head. I try to say, 'Not the tramp. Not the Barns.' But no words come out, only howling as infantile as Milly's in her pushchair. I'm behaving just like that poor ghost in the grave – brave once, brave twice, but not brave for ever.

My father puts his arms round me. My mother strokes my hair.

'Poor kid,' says Geoff.

'You'll have to report it,' murmurs my mother over my head to my father when I quieten a little.

'Have we got the telephone number of the police station?' murmurs my father, and at once I begin to howl again more hopelessly than ever.

Someone's knocking at the front door. Terror silences my howling – the police are here already.

Geoff goes downstairs to answer it.

'It's Barbara Berrill,' he says when he comes back. 'Can Stephen come out to play?'

I resume my howling.

I'm woken from the depths of a deep and dreamless sleep by the uneasy feeling that something's wrong.

I lie in the darkness, listening to the sound of Geoff's breathing, trying to work out what it is.

The pain in my throat – yes. And when I put my fingers to my throat to investigate, I find the bandage round my neck. Now I remember – *everything*'s wrong: Milly's weeping, Dee's pressing her hands to her ears, Keith's intent face in front of mine . . .

The policeman who'll be coming in the morning to talk to me . . . The scarf that the policeman will find when he comes . . .

Yes, where is it? I sit up in bed in a panic. I can't remember what I've done with it! I've left it lying around somewhere for anyone to find!

I scrabble under the pillow, my heart cold . . . No, there it is, just where I shoved it, smeared with dried blood, when my mother put me to bed and I at last opened my clenched hand. At once I see the policeman searching the bedroom, opening the toy cupboard, turning back the bedding . . . I'll have to find somewhere better to hide it.

Is this what woke me? Possibly. Or is there something else wrong? Something I still can't quite locate?

Something in the room? Or something outside?

I get up and put my head under the blackout blind. It's as dark outside as it is in, and it takes me a long time to distinguish even the roofline of the houses opposite against the sky. What I'm peering into is what Keith and I were waiting for: the dark of the moon.

And in that blackness there's some kind of lurking presence. A sound of some kind. A very small sound, but one that shouldn't be there. I listen hard. It's steady and unchanging, a faint, sustained sibilance, as if some creature were quietly and inexhaustibly exhaling.

I begin to shiver, because I know that I have to go out there into the breathing darkness to find somewhere to hide the scarf. I quietly put on my sandals and pull a jumper over my pyjamas, as I did before. I remember, almost wistfully, that earlier night when the moon was full, and my childish feeling that I'd need a knotted rope to climb out of the window. The difficulty in getting out this time, though, is not one that ropes could solve. The difficulty is the darkness itself and the sound in the darkness that shouldn't be there. The difficulty is the shivering that won't stop.

Once again I ease back the bolt on the kitchen door, then edge my way step by step through the confusions of the front garden, and stand at the gate in the perfumed and empty stillness of the street, wondering which way to go, as insubstantial as the darkness enclosing me. The sound's more insistent out here. It seems to come from far off, and yet to be in the air all around me. For a moment I think I hear muffled, distant voices calling, but when I hold my breath and still my shivering so as to be certain, there's nothing but the same long sigh as before.

Where am I going to find a hiding place? I can't lock the scarf away inside the trunk, because Keith will find it there even if the policeman doesn't. I think of each dark house along the street in turn. The Sheldons, the Stotts . . . Lamorna, Trewinnick . . . Each one's a world closed against me.

The voices again . . . Again I hold my breath and try not to shiver . . . Nothing. Only that long, unnatural animal breath.

There's one possibility I can think of, and I stand there for a long time in the darkness before I can persuade myself to accept it. But if there's nowhere else . . . I walk to the end of the street and turn towards the tunnel.

As I get closer my dread increases. The pitch darkness of the tunnel mouth is bad enough, but there's something else about it as well – something that's changed. The mass of the embankment towering against the darkness of the sky above me as I approach seems somehow wrong. I have the impression that there's even more of it than usual pressing down upon the mouth of the brickwork. Something about its outline seems different, too. The horizon between the blackness of the sky above it is no longer even and level – it's jagged and confused.

The whole sound and shape of the world has become in some way dislocated.

Now I'm enclosed by the hollow darkness beneath this strange mass . . . feeling my way along the slime through the huge echoes of my own breathing . . . and emerging into that same level, quiet breathing of the night. It reminds me, as I bend back the rusty links of the fence, of the level breathing of the unseen man behind me when I was here before, and once again I feel the cold prickling in the nape of my neck.

I climb through the gap, and fumble my way forward on my hands and knees through the stalks of cow parsley until I find the hollow behind the brickwork where the croquet box was hidden. I take the scarf out of the sleeve of my jumper, and bury it as best I can in the dark under the loose, dank earth and the rank vegetation.

A new sound makes me raise my head. Distant barking. There's someone in the Lanes.

That poor sick ghost has risen from his grave. He's coming to punish my betrayal of him – coming to catch me in the very act of burying the precious object he trusted me to deliver. I scramble out of the undergrowth, and through the gap in the fence. I run back towards the tunnel, then stop, because something's entering it at the other end. Two dim grids of hooded light and their two reflections in the puddles come towards me, bucking slowly in counterpoint over the unevenness of the track. The howl of an engine in low gear echoes around the brickwork.

A vehicle of some sort – and in the middle of the night, in a place where no vehicle has ever been seen before.

There's nowhere it can be going except to the Barns.

I crawl back through the fence and wait behind the brickwork for it to pass. They're coming for him. They're coming for him because I let myself be bullied once again, even if this time I didn't give in, and because I've been too weak and inept to conceal the fact from my parents. And there's nothing I can do about it. All I can do is hide yet again.

I wait, sick at myself, for the murmur of the engine to die away.

It continues, though, as quiet and steady as that mysterious breathing.

I raise my head an inch or two above the brickwork. There's the vehicle, stationary in front of me, a vague, murmuring bulk outlined against the faintly illuminated patch of ground in front of the blacked-out headlights at one end and the small red glow from the hooded tail light at the other. A pair of doors stand open at the back, and two small splashes of light are dancing about over the retaining wall opposite and the embankment above it.

One of the splashes swings abruptly across to my side of the lane, and I drop below the top of the brickwork just as the dazzle of the beam reaches me.

I'm wrong. It's not him they've come for. It's me.

The torch finds the gap in the fence. I press myself face down in the hollow where I've hidden the scarf, as I did once before, and I hear the catch of the wire on cloth as someone squeezes through. A man's breath. Then the snagging of the wire again, and the sound of a second man.

The rough hands are just about to seize me and drag me out into the blinding of their torches . . .

The breathing and the breaking of the undergrowth come closer . . . then move past me and grow quieter. I hear the scrape of boots on brickwork. The men have scrambled up on to the parapet, as Keith and I did the first time we came here, and they're following it up towards the top of the tunnel mouth.

It's not me they're looking for, then. Or will they come back down if I move, and find me as Keith and I came back down and found the box?

I wait . . . wait . . .

The barking of the dogs has long ceased. Whoever it is coming along the Lanes is now well away from the cottages. I can almost feel his approach . . . Or has he seen the lights of the van already, and stopped?

Still I wait. Still there's nothing to be heard but the murmur of the waiting vehicle and the quiet unnatural breathing of the night. I slowly lift my head above the brickwork . . .

And now I hear voices in the Lanes, and at the same time see torches approaching along the top of the embankment. Not two now but half a dozen of them, coming slowly along the ganger's path beside the rails. Every now and then one of the beams swings sideways and lights up the wheels and undersides of the long train of stationary trucks waiting on the up line, all the way across the top of the tunnel and on towards the cutting. One of the beams swings upwards for a moment and catches part of the cargo projecting from them – the duck-egg blue underside of a shattered aircraft wing with its red, white and blue roundel, sticking up from a jagged tangle of scrap metal, a camouflage-painted tailplane with its red, white and blue flash.

I hide my head again as the men come scrambling and slithering slowly down the sloping parapet of the retaining wall above me. They're breathing hard now, and uttering little grunts of warning and acknowledgement as they struggle with the weight and awkwardness of the load they're carrying. They all wait, three feet away from me, breathing and shifting, as the wire fence is ripped off the concrete posts, and goes rustling back to allow the bearers and their burden to pass.

The voices approaching from the Lanes call out. 'Got him?' says one of them.

'Most of him,' gasps one of the bearers. 'Want to look?'

A silence, and then, on the other side of the brickwork, the helpless groan and gagging of someone who's turned aside to vomit.

The one thing I know for sure is that *I* did this. I wept and was weak and said nothing, and they went to fetch him. He fled before them on to the railway embankment, and ran down the line, home towards the houses in the Close, or up it and out to the great wide world. And there in the darkness, I suppose, he missed his footing. At once the terrible secret force hidden in the rail leapt out at him, and the passing trains cut him in pieces.

The doors of the vehicle slam to. The murmur of the engine rises to a howl, then slowly, joltingly recedes, and echoes through the tunnel. The voices go echoing after it, some of them now raised in a cacophony of ghostly calls and answering laughter.

The noises die away, until once again there's no sound left in the darkness but that same unsettling, long drawn-out sigh. I know what it is now: the hiss of steam escaping from the locomotive halted way up ahead in the depths of the cutting. The sigh gathers itself together into a single sharp exhalation. Another exhalation – a flurry of exhalations – a measured sequence of them – and the clanking of tightened couplings comes spreading back down the line of trucks. Slowly the train resumes its interrupted progress up the gradient.

By the time I'm back in my bed it's dissolved into the remoteness of the night, and the blackness is silent again.

The game's finally over.

11

Everything in the Close is as it was; and everything has changed. The houses sit where they sat, but everything they once said they say no longer.

Not to me, at any rate. I walk up the road and back once more, stupidly, a stranger who's beginning to make himself more than a little conspicuous, a confused old man wandering the streets. I turn the corner and walk under the railway bridge again, even more stupidly, since there's nothing left of the Lanes at all. Where in this labyrinth of Crescents, Walks, and Meads was the sycamore with the rotted rope? Where was the dried-up pond, where were the Cottages? Was this dull service station next to the roundabout once by any chance the Barns?

I retrace my steps to the railway bridge. It's still flanked on either side by brick retaining walls, as the old tunnel was. I walk along the smooth grey pavement, peering at the brickwork on the side where the croquet box was hidden. The walls must have been rebuilt when they replaced the tunnel and widened the road. Or is it possible that the old wall might have been kept on one side of the road for economy's sake? The bricks here look well weathered . . . the gradient of the capping course seems familiar . . . At the low end of the wall now, where the rusty wire fence was, is an electricity substation, with a clean new galvanised wire fence boxing it off from the embankment beyond. There's no way of crawling through it, and it's too high for me to climb. I peer through the serviceable grey links. The bottom of the embankment behind the wall has been used as a tip, and it's impossible to see, under the layers of ancient rubbish, whether there's any gap behind the brickwork where something might be hidden.

I feel small, unreasonable disappointment. I'm embarrassed to confess it, even to myself, but I think this may be why I've stopped to look at the bridge. It may be why I've come on this whole expedition. Just to make sure. Just to check – and this is too silly to think, as soon as I put it into words – just to check that it's not still here somewhere. The scarf. The one piece of material evidence there might still be that the whole strange dream actually happened.

I know perfectly well, of course, that it can't possibly have survived. It would have rotted half a century ago. If it wasn't found by somebody first. Other children, perhaps, pursuing some fantasy of their own. I wonder what they'd have made of it. Chemnitz . . . Leipzig . . . Zwickau . . . By the time it was found all three would have been in either the Soviet zone of occupation or the German Democratic Republic, and it might have suggested Communist spying rather than Nazi. I imagine them carrying it importantly off to the police, or taking it with proper scholastic curiosity for identification in the local museum. I might just possibly find it still preserved in some forgotten dusty box, or displayed in a glass case along with a dutiful assemblage of shrapnel and old ration books.

Why didn't I go back later and recover it myself? Because from that night on I was in a different corridor of my life. A door had closed behind me, and I never opened it again. I never went back to the Lanes. I never walked through the tunnel. I put all those things out of my head. Until today. Squeezed in here between the substation and the galvanised wire fence, and thinking these ancient thoughts, I'm standing on this particular spot of ground for the first time in over fifty years.

So what did happen after than night? Nothing. Life went on. I got up next morning as usual, so far as I remember. I went to school, and struggled to keep my attention fixed upon the algebra and history exams. I refused to satisfy everyone's curiosity about the bandage round my throat, and endured as philosophically as I could the hypothesis eventually offered by my friends Hanning and Neale – that I had attempted to hang myself, but had failed because I was too weeny, too weedy, and too Wheatley. To my parents I said nothing about the events of the night. They said nothing further to me about the injury to my throat, and no policeman came to question me. It seemed to be understood that somehow the problem had been solved, and that I needn't be tormented further. I suppose there must have been an inquest on the body that had been found on the line, and there must have been evidence of identification, but I can't remember hearing about it. Well, it was wartime. Not everything was reported or spoken about.

Life continued; but on a slightly different course. I never went to Keith's house again, I never went back to the lookout. I don't know what became of the bayonet any more than I do of the scarf. Perhaps that's in a museum, too.

Every now and then I saw Keith cycling past on his way to school or back, but he didn't notice me. I caught the odd glimpse of his father as he worked in the front garden, and heard him whistling a passage or two from the great cadenza that never ended. Sometimes his mother would smile at me as she passed carrying her shopping basket, or letters to post, a cravat still high on her throat long after my bandages had gone. Once she stopped and said I must come to tea again some time, but 'some time' was never any particular day, and very soon Keith went away, first on holiday with his family and then to start boarding school.

Auntie Dee always smiled at me too, as bravely as ever, but my mother told me that she was really terribly upset, because Uncle Peter had been posted missing, and because, just when she most needed the support of her family, she'd apparently had some kind of falling out with Keith's mother. My mother sometimes tried to help with Milly and the shopping, until Auntie Dee moved out of the district a few weeks later, after which no one ever saw her again. My mother had been a little bit soft on Uncle Peter herself, she once confided to me – all the wives in the Close had.

I called at Lamorna several times, but Barbara could never come out to play. I began to see her across the road at the Averys.

Charlie Avery had been called up, and Dave would be working on the three-wheeler on his own – with Barbara sitting cross-legged on the driveway watching him and handing him tools, her purse with the bobbly blue leather and the shiny popper still slung around her neck. I went through the first of the agonies which I was going to discover later were usual on these occasions.

The scent of the limes and the honeysuckle faded; the treacly, reassuring breath of the buddleia came and went; the raw urgent reek of the privet faded.

There were many things that Keith had been wrong about, I realised gradually as life went on. But about one thing, and one quite surprising thing, he'd been right, though it took me several years to recognise it. There was a German spy in the Close that summer. It wasn't his mother – it was me.

Everything is as it was; and everything has changed. Stephen Wheatley has become this old man, treading slowly and warily in the footsteps of his former self, and the name of this old man is Stefan Weitzler. That undersized observer in the privet, spying on the comings and goings of the street, has reverted to the name under which he was registered in the peaceful green district of the great German city where he was born.

I was reborn as Stephen when my parents left Germany in 1935. My mother was English anyway, and she'd always spoken English to us at home, but now my father became more English still, and we all turned into Wheatleys. She died at the beginning of the 1960s, and when my father followed her less than a year later I felt a great restlessness stirring in me – the converse of that same restlessness that's brought me back now to the Close. It's the longing to be elsewhere that in Germany we call *Fernweh* which is in my case also *Heimweh*, a longing to be home – the terrible pull of opposites that torments the displaced everywhere.

Well, my life in England had somehow never really taken flight. My marriage was never quite a real marriage, my job in the engineering department of the local polytechnic was never quite a real job. I felt a yearning to know more about my father, about where he'd grown up, where he and my mother had fallen in love, where I'd first seen the light. So I went to take a look, and I discovered that my first two years had been spent in a quiet, garden-lined street that seemed to be a dreamlike echo of the Close in which I later grew up, which is no doubt why the Close itself always seemed to be a dreamlike echo in its turn.

I had a bleak few months in my rediscovered homeland, struggling with a language I'd only started to learn in my adolescence, too late to be ever quite at ease with, working in an environment I couldn't quite understand. Of my father's past scarcely a trace remained. His parents and two brothers had all been taken and murdered. His sister had for some reason been left, and instead had been killed in her own cellar, along with her own two children, by Uncle Peter, or by his colleagues in Bomber Command.

And yet, and yet . . . I stayed. My temporary job somehow became a permanent one. I don't suppose you've ever read the English-language installation and maintenance manuals for Siemens transformers and high-voltage switchgear, but if by any chance you have then you're familiar with at any rate some of my work. The story in the manuals, it occurs to me, is once again somebody else's, just as the story of the German spy, and all the other stories of my childhood, were Keith's. Once again all I've done is play the loyal disciple.

And of course the day came when I met someone else, and as I began to see Germany through her familiar eyes, my perception of everything around me changed once again . . . Soon there was a house, in another quiet, tree-lined street . . . The house became a home . . . There were children, and many German in-laws to visit . . . And now, before I can sort out whether I belong here or there, or even which is here and which is there, my children are grown up, and we have their mother's grave to tend each week.

* * *

Actually there were *two* German spies in the Close, now I come to think about it – and the other one was a serious and dedicated professional.

I once tried to gain a little credit with Keith by claiming that my father was a German spy. Well, so he was, I discovered later. At any rate he was a German, and he had some kind of job in economic intelligence, though he was on the British side, not the German. This was why he came back when he did from that mysterious 'business trip' of his to the North. They gave him an early release from his internment as an enemy alien in the Isle of Man because they needed his knowledge of the German optical industry, and his ability to understand decrypts relating to it. Someone who'd worked on the history of the Allied bombing campaign once told me that if it hadn't been for the work of his department, the Germans would have been better supplied with gunsights, and Uncle Peter and his colleagues would have had a harder time still with German anti-aircraft defences.

I suppose I've got more and more like my father as I've got older. I hear myself saying the same irritatingly eccentric things he used to say, that I never realised at the time were simply plain, ordinary German. I'd look into my son's bedroom when he was a child and tell him off for the frightful *Kuddelmuddel*, and when he tried to offer some excuse I'd snap that it was nonsense, just as my father would have done: *Schnickschnack*!

Yes, we were the Germans, in a country at war with them, and no one ever knew it. No one except me overheard the pleas of the desperate fellow-refugees who came to my father for help. No one else guessed what language they were speaking together. We were also the Juice, in a juiceless district (the mysterious dark strangers at Trewinnick turned out to be Orthodox Greeks) and no one ever knew that, either. I'm no more religious than my father ever was, but I too have vexed my family with that same residual conviction that Friday evening, when the first star is ventured upon the sky, was a time for all of us to stay home and be together.

Why did my parents conceal all this? I suppose they wanted to make things easier for Geoff and me. Maybe it did at the time, too. Keith's parents would have probably never have allowed me inside their house if they'd known what we were. Later, though, when I found out, it made things harder. For me, though apparently not for Geoff, who was four years more German than me but four times more British. He knew where we came from – he was already six when we left. Or at any rate he sort of knew, he told me much later, in the way we sort of know so many things. Why didn't he tell me at the time? I imagine because what he also knew from the reticence of my parents, and knew for sure, was that there were some things that must never be talked about.

No, I think it went deeper than that. I think what he instinctively grasped was this: that some things must never even be known.

Geoff Wheatley he remained, anyway, and never thought of going back to being Joachim Weitzler. He married, moved to a house much like our old one in the Close and less than a mile away from it, lived out his life as a local auctioneer and valuer, kept up his early interest in girls and smoking, got into various rather unappetising marital scrapes, and died of lung cancer, with much suffering but, so far as I know, no great anxieties about his past. Not, at any rate, ones that he ever confided to me. He'd even carefully forgotten all his German. Or so I supposed. Once, though, when I visited him in the hospice as he lay dying, he seemed to think in his confusion that I was our father. He took my hand, and when I bent close to his lips what he called me was not 'Daddy' which we'd always called our father in the time I remembered, but '*Papi*'. And what he kept saying, in a little frightened voice, was that he was frightened of the dark: '*Papi, Papi, ich hab' Angst vor dem Dunkeln.*'

What happened to all the other children in the street? The McAfees' son died in a Japanese prisoner-of-war camp. Charlie Avery lost an eye and a hand in a training exercise two months after he was called up. I've no idea what became of Barbara Berrill. I think Keith's a barrister of some sort. I saw his name on a doorway in the Inner Temple when I was getting my divorce. 'Mr K. R. G. Hayward' – there can't be more than one Mr K. R. G. Hayward, can there? I nearly went in and confronted him. Why didn't I? Some last residual fear, perhaps. That was thirty years ago – he's probably a judge by now. I can imagine him as a judge. Or perhaps he's retired. I can imagine him retired, too, tending his roses and whistling.

Or else he's dead. Can I imagine him dead? Not really. Can I imagine myself, for that matter, lying in my narrow grave, with that same terrible intensity as I imagined it then? No. The imagination ages, like everything else. The intensity fades. You don't get as afraid as you used to.

I walk up the street once more, to get full value from my air fare. One last look before someone calls the police or the local social services. Lamorna, I see, is now simply No. 6. Would the murmur of 'Number Six' ever have got as confused with the scent of the privet as the soft syllables of 'Lamorna' did? The entanglement of wild roses in the front garden there has been replaced by a few small beds of pansies at the edge of the gravel drive, and a white-haired old lady is kneeling to weed them. She glances up at me, and I suddenly realise, with the most terrible jolt of recognition, of hope and dismay, that it's Barbara.

She looks indifferently at me for a moment, and then returns to her weeding. It's not Barbara. Of course it's not. I don't think it is.

In any case, what I'm really thinking about isn't Barbara – or Keith, for that matter – or any of the others. It's that scarf still. It keeps nagging at me. I should just like to know for sure what happened to that, if nothing else.

Not that there's much chance it would offer many surprises, even if I could get my hands on it and unfold it at last. I know exactly what I should see printed on the silk: a map of Germany, and the rest of Europe as far west as the channel coast – not the landscape that any German might want to spy on, or to bomb, or to parachute into. It was the escape map that all *British* aircrew routinely carried in the pocket of their flying jackets, in the remote hope that if that if they were shot down they might somehow try to find their way home.

Did I really not know at the time that the broken man in the Barns was Uncle Peter? Of course I knew. I knew as soon as he called me by name. No, before that. As soon as I heard him behind me in the moonlight. Or much earlier still, even. From the very beginning, perhaps. Just as he himself had always known that *she* was really the one. *Always her . . . From the very beginning . . .* When was the very beginning, for him and her? Perhaps from the afternoon when he and the nice jolly girl he'd just met at some local tennis club found themselves making up a foursome for doubles with her composed a tranquil elder sister and her sister's unsociable, middle-aged husband. *Always her.* Even as he'd stood in front of the church door in his RAF uniform later, with the wrong sister on his arm.

And yet probably he hadn't known at all, any more than I did about him. I went on thinking, even after I'd heard him speak, that he was a *German.* This was what I clung on to – that he was a *German.* His Germanness hung in the air, as pervasive and as transforming as the scent of the privet or the sound of Lamorna. Whatever I secretly knew, and whenever I knew it, I also understood that it was something that must never be known.

I look up at the sky, as I did when I arrived; the one enduring feature of the street. I think of the uncontrollable terror seizing him, ten thousand feet up there in the dark emptiness, and five hundred miles from here. And I think of the terror that must have seized my aunt and her children, too, as the unbreathable gases from the burning house filled their dark cellar ten thousand feet below him, or someone like him.

I think of the shame that pursued him afterwards, from which he fled into that dark pit. At least my aunt and her children were spared the shame.

What we did to each other in those few years of madness! What we did to ourselves!

Now all the mysteries have been resolved, or as resolved as they're ever likely to be. All that remains is the familiar slight ache in the bones, like an old wound when the weather changes. *Heimweh* or *Fernweh*? A longing to be there or a longing to be here, even though I'm here already? Or to be both at once? Or to be neither, but in the old country of the past, that will never be reached again in either place?

Time to go. So, once again – thank you, everyone. Thank you for having me.

And, on the air as I turn the corner at the end of the street, a sudden faint breath of something familiar. Something sweet, coarse, and intimately unsettling.

Even here, after all. Even now.

The best in classic and

Jane Austen

Elizabeth Laird

Beverley Naidoo   Roddy Doyle

Robert Swindells

George Orwell

Charles Dickens

Charlotte Brontë

Jan Mark

Anne Fine

Anthony Horowitz